# STRONGER THAN STEEL

OTHER BOOKS BY R.C. SPROUL

# Stronger Than Steel

The Wayne Alderson Story

*R. C. Sproul*

1817

**Harper & Row, Publishers, San Francisco**

Cambridge, Hagerstown, Philadelphia, New York
London, Mexico City, São Paulo, Sydney

FIRST EDITION

*Designer: Jim Mennick*

Library of Congress Cataloging in Publication Data

Sproul, Robert Charles, 1939–
  Stronger than steel.

  1. Alderson, Wayne. 2. Church and labor—United
States. 3. Industrial relations—United States.
4. Business consultants—United States—Biography.
I. Title.
HD6338.2.U5S67  1980      658.3′14      80–7746
ISBN 0–06–067502–0

80 81 82 83 84 10 9 8 7 6 5 4 3 2 1

## Special Dedication

To Charles "Red" Preston and to the men of Pittron
and to all who labor and to all who manage.

WAYNE ALDERSON

# Contents

# Preface

This is not an ordinary biography. It is the story of a man's life, but it is also the story of a movement that has sparked unprecedented excitement in the arena of labor and management relations. It is about the quest for dignity in the workplace, and how the Value of the Person movement provides a model for those seeking a more excellent way.

There are many different ways to write a biography. One may be coldly professional, wielding the pen as one would wield a surgeon's scalpel, to cut with precision into the ugly portions of the human viscera. One may approach the subject academically, using carefully noted documentation that makes the reading far more accurate—and usually far less interesting. Still another approach is to probe the psyche of the subject, reducing him to an object of psychoanalytical determinism. All of these methods preclude, to a large degree, the author's personal and emotional involvement with the character he is describing.

These are not the methods I have chosen. They would be artificial, and thus they would not work. Wayne Alderson is a friend and a co-worker. I am as caught up in his struggle as he is; so I am able to write from his viewpoint, to get close to his heartbeat. I am writing about a common man with uncommon courage, a man whom I honestly believe to be one of the most courageous human beings I've ever encountered. Because of my respect for the man, it has been hard for me to write of his all-too-human shortcomings. But my commitment to the man should not negate the truth of the portrait. Indeed, friendship often allows one to benefit from a second glance, to see virtue where others see only vice, to see strengths which, from a distance, may appear to be weaknesses.

I leave the task of historical research or technical analysis to others. Perhaps the demythologzing is best left to the next generation, who I suspect will still be grappling with the significance of Wayne Alderson. As the author of this book, I have had to write myself out of the story, even though I lived a significant part of it.

Gratitude is in order for the help given by numerous people. Special gratitude must be expressed to the people at Harper & Row who believed in the project, especially Clayton E. Carlson, the publisher, and Roy M. Carlisle, my editor. Acknowledgment must also be given to Jack Bleriot of WIIC TV in Pittsburgh, Mrs. John Hartwell Hillman, and Dr. Hilda Kring, for their suggestions for revisions. Thanks also to Kathy Constantine and Joann Goebel for typing several drafts of the manuscript and to the hostesses and waitresses of the Holiday Inn in Ligonier, Pennsylvania, for allowing us to use a table in their restaurant as an office.

R. C. SPROUL

*The Ligonier Valley*
*May 1980*

# I

## Point Man

Thy soul shall find itself alone
Mid dark thoughts of the gray tombstone
Not one, of all the crowd, to pry
Into thine hour of secrecy.
EDGAR ALLEN POE
*"Spirits of the Dead"*

Wayne Alderson gazed across the landscape and thought it was a ghostly place to be, a Stygian plain haunted by endless rows of pallid crosses, a place suitable for burial. Yet there was something contradictory about the setting. On the surface the scene was tranquil, quietly elegant: the manicured grass, the symmetry of the straight rows of white markers extending into the horizon, and the silence of the day, interrupted only sporadically by the fluting of the birds or the monotonous humming of a lawnmower. This was a mirage appropriate for death, the cosmetic that covered one of the world's most grotesque blemishes—the hideous holocaust of World War II.

Beneath the surface of this carefully groomed plot of real estate were collected the broken remains of 10,489 men who perished violently on the battlefields of Europe. This was the Lorraine American Cemetery in St. Avold, France—the largest

American military burial ground on the continent, narrowly exceeding in quantity the crosses planted in the earth at Normandy. Unlike Flanders, no colorful fields of poppies lent hue to the bleakness of the scene; the austerity of St. Avold gave mute testimony to the finality of death.

This summer day in 1974 found the American businessman staring at the crosses—row after row after row of albino crosses. He had traveled thousands of miles to be here, but his purpose was not that of the typical American tourist on a pleasure trip. This man was not here for pleasure: he was here to pay a debt, to keep a rendezvous with his own personal history. Although compelled to be here, he was in no hurry. He knew that in the sea of crosses before him, one bore the name of a man who had been waiting for him silently for almost thirty years. He was troubled by the conviction that the name on that cross should have been his own, *WAYNE T. ALDERSON*.

Alderson is an anomaly, an enigma even to those who know him well. He is a man who does not "know his place," because his place has no sharp definition. He is at once businessman and laborer, alleycat and pussycat, cultured and crass, gentle and vehement, religious and profane. He is a coal miner's son who became a corporate executive, a soldier who became a peacemaker, an idealist who lives like a pragmatist.

His appearance that day reflected his contradictory nature. His angular, chiseled face was that of a laborer, but his clothes belonged to a top-level executive. His suit was carefully tailored, bearing the logo of Pierre Cardin. But while the clothes fit the body, they seemed incongruous on the man. Sandy-haired, his razor-cut style somehow gave a boyish look to the nearly fifty-year-old man. Alderson looked like a grown-up Tom Sawyer.

His face seemed set in steel, but his deep blue eyes unveiled a sorrowful soul. They were the eyes of a man who had seen too much pain. Baleful, ethereal, almost vacant, Wayne's eyes startled people and made them wonder what he had seen that had affected him so strongly.

Normally, the lanky Alderson walked with rapid, ungainly strides, moving quickly with his chin jutting into the wind. But today his pace was measured, his movements hesitant: he had a promise to keep. Alderson was on a sacred mission, the fulfillment of a pact sealed in blood.

He was flanked by his wife and daughter, both of whom shared the name Nancy and the same Swedish blonde hair. His loved ones were there to support him, and to learn for themselves something of what the man had experienced. The family stood gazing at the landscape whitened by crosses. They all knew what they were looking for: a grave modestly marked with a name and two dates, *1923–1945;* one name on a single cross lost somewhere in the seemingly endless rows.

Confounded by the size of the cemetary, the Aldersons walked to the information office. There they found the caretaker, who explained in broken English that, in recent years, visitors to the cemetery were almost exclusively tourists. The days of visits from next-of-kin and friends of the men buried there had faded into the past. Memory of the war had dimmed and the living were preoccupied with the present. The caretaker seemed to sense the drama of this occasion. He knew that this visit was different, and he wanted to participate in the Alderson pilgrimage.

The Frenchman escorted the Aldersons first to a private rose bed, where he cut flowers suitable for adorning a grave. As they walked through the cemetary, Alderson gripped the flowers like an awkward teenager bearing a bouquet for his first date. At last he moved away from the group, approaching the designated site alone. Excited, yet apprehensive, he focused his attention on the cross, aware of nothing but the name he read there: *PRESTON—CHARLES.*

Involuntarily, Alderson sank to his knees and spoke with quivering voice to the silent grave.

"It's been a long time, friend."

Nancy and Nancy Jean walked up behind him and placed understanding hands on his stooped shoulders. Nothing was said, but all silently thought the words of the New Testament: "Greater love has no man than this, that he lay down his life for his friend."

More than one of Alderson's friends was interred in this place, but Charles Preston had literally fulfilled the words of Jesus nearly thirty years earlier, just across the border in Germany. Unbidden, Alderson's thoughts drifted back to the events that had provoked this summer pilgrimage to St. Avold.

*FEBRUARY 1945.* When he arrived at the front at Colmar in the Alsace Lorraine region of France, Wayne Alderson was the classic green recruit panting for action. At eighteen years of age he brought to the battlefields of Europe an unbridled thirst for the glory of war. Newsclips, parades, and Hollywood had done their job in pumping the boy full of excitement for the epic heroism of combat. He was ready . . . more than ready. He couldn't wait. He knew the war was winding down to a close, now that El Alamein and Omaha Beach were already history. He was afraid he might be too late and the war would pass him by. But, in the next weeks, Wayne Alderson would find that enough war remained to fill a lifetime, and the boy in him would be rudely pushed into manhood.

A few days after Wayne arrived at the front, his company commander issued a call of assembly. Heavy casualties from firefights, snipers, and artillery bombardments featuring the feared "88s" (88 millimeter cannon shells) had thinned their ranks. The company's advance scouts had both been killed, and the commander was looking for replacements.

"I need a point man."

These words had an effect on the men similar to the command "eyes right!"—only now, most eyes were fixed on the ground. They shuffled their feet in embarrassed silence, hoping someone else would volunteer. To be a point man is to accept one of the most dangerous assignments of war, to face a task that carries one of the shortest life-expectancies of any infantryman.

The fate of their previous scouts had reinforced the grim statistics.

The point man serves his unit as their advance scout. He must isolate himself from the main body, proceeding alone in front of the troops. His job is to observe, penetrate, and probe the placements of the enemy, leading both reconnaissance and combat patrols. The point man has often been described as a man who "has more guts than brains," because he is usually the first person exposed to enemy activity, and thus often the first casualty of combat. The point man frequently serves as a human mine sweeper and is the prime target for enemy sniper fire. His task is of extreme importance to the main body of men; he is their eyes and their ears. If a patrol or platoon can't trust their scout, their commitment falters. The job is as critical as it is deadly.

"I need a point man," the captain repeated. But he didn't have to wait long for a response. This was the job the boy had left home to do. The words were out of his mouth before he knew it.

"I'll go," he volunteered, and stepped forward.

At that moment Wayne Alderson stepped into a role which was to characterize the rest of his life.

"You're crazy, you stupid son of a bitch! Why did you volunteer? Now I have to do it too. If you go, I go."

With these words of protest, Charles "Red" Preston volunteered as second scout to back up Alderson. Wayne and Red were friends, their close comradery cemented by the adhesive of war. Red's nickname was inevitable—his hair was a brilliant auburn-chestnut, the color some women try to capture from a bottle. His skin was fair, and splashed with freckles. Small-boned and slight of build, Red was wiry and radiated life. In his dress uniform, he drew girls like a magnet. Red was quiet, but he was never afraid to voice his carefully thought out opinions. On a weekend pass with the guys he was fun-loving, rather than rowdy and earned a reputation as a bit of a "screw-off." Playing Huck Finn to Alderson's Sawyer, he raised the eyebrows of some of the older veterans. Wary of this free-living recruit, they warned Wayne, "Don't let Red back you up on point. He'll get you killed. When the heat's on, screw-offs like that turn and run."

Stubbornly Wayne replied, "Hey, it's my life . . . I want Red."

So the boys became scouts, and the men withheld their judgment until they had the opportunity to measure them under fire.

The veterans had known Red longer than Wayne had, yet the instant rapport the two scouts had sensed when they met only a few days earlier made them feel as if they had known each other all of their lives. Red was the first soldier Wayne met when he came to the front as a replacement, and it was Red who, in his role of big brother to the rookie Alderson, taught him some of his tricks of survival.

At this time the American forces were dug in on the French side of the Rhine River, consolidating their recent victory at Colmar. The Germans had retreated across the Rhine to set up their defense perimeter on its banks. At night, their crack patrols stealthily crossed the river, penetrating the American lines, capturing isolated GI's and silently killing others with commando-style knife attacks. The information the patrols secured about American pillbox and artillery placements resulted in daily heavy bombardments across the river. Because of the heavy toll these shellings took on the U.S. forces, the American commander assembled a small force to hold counter raids into the German side. The first such raid was Alderson's baptism as a point man.

At precisely midnight, Wayne and Red pushed their rubber raft off from the French shore, moving silently across the water. Clouds obscured the moon, giving them the desired cover of darkness. As they neared the enemy shore, they could hear the voices of the soldiers manning the German flak station, and, in spite of the darkness, they could make out silhouettes of guard patrols on the riverbank.

Abruptly, cruelly, the clouds parted and the rubber raft was bathed in moonlight. The scouts were terrified; they felt as if they were under a spotlight at the mouth of the German camp. Red whispered quickly, "Let's get the hell out of here," as they started to paddle furiously in retreat. The German guards, probably alerted by the splashing paddles, spotted the scouts and opened fire. As bullets zinged off the water around them and tracers lit the sky, Wayne and Red threw their equipment overboard to lighten their load for a swifter retreat. The Americans answered the German offensive from their shore, opening with cover fire to protect their vulnerable scouts. Midway across the river a loud hissing sound signaled a direct hit on the raft. With the flimsy boat sinking in the murky water, Wayne and Red began to swim for their lives. They were fished out by a grinning veteran named Billy Weaver, who pulled them to safety saying, "You guys picked a hell of a time for a moonlight swim in the Rhine!"

Billy Weaver was a tall, sinewy veteran from a coal-mining town in Pennsylvania. In his late twenties, he became the older brother to both Wayne and Red. After rescuing them from the Rhine that night, he took a personal interest in the younger scouts, sticking up for them with the older men. Billy had already seen too much war. He sensed that final victory was in sight and mused often about the end. He said, "Wouldn't it be great to wake up some morning and look across the Rhine and see the Russians over there?" Weaver didn't care about politics; he just wanted to see the Germans defeated.

"Point men out!"

With this command, the war became real. Wayne came to fear this order more than any. Out there, he was alone, with nothing and no one to hide behind. He felt as if he were stripped naked. Nothing was in front of him but the enemy and death; behind him the men watched to see how he handled himself. At first, however, his greatest fear was that he would show fear.

It didn't take long for real fear to hit. There in the dirt in front of him was a body. He saw the Nazi uniform, a swastika, a gun belt, a tarnished helmet. What had once been human flesh was showing signs of decay, the enemy's body was already starting to bloat. The boy's war was now with his own stomach. It hadn't looked like this in the John Wayne films. All glamour vanished. Now, as adventure turned to caution, an instinct for survival overwhelmed his desire for excitement. He fought to keep himself from screaming.

His fear was so great, he wanted to un-volunteer. But his fear of being thought a coward was stronger than his fear of death, so he ranged out farther from the company. His shoes seemed to weigh a ton as he put more distance between himself and his unit.

Red warned Wayne not to go so far, but he kept going. He knew that the further out he roamed, the greater respect he would earn from the men. The more courage he displayed, the more protection he could expect from his troops. This gave him a false sense of security, a quixotic feeling of safety.

Alderson got the reward he craved from his captain.

"Slim, you're really exposed out there. That's the way it should be. The men know they can trust you."

Wayne sensed the captain was manipulating him, psyching up the youthful volunteer to keep him in his place, but he didn't care. The approval of combat-hardened veterans meant more to him than his own safety.

Alderson went out on the point almost daily for weeks, and each time he made it back unharmed. He had equipped himself for a one-man war, bending the rules that regulated normal issue of weapons to a scout. First he exchanged his standard M-1 rifle for a Thompson submachine gun. The tommy-gun became his friend. Alderson was still a kid, playing the role of a comic book hero. He made his forays into the enemy's position loaded down with extra ammo and grenades. Scrounging thirty-load clips instead of twenty-load, Alderson kept himself supplied with fifty percent more firepower than he should have had. Fully armed, his ammo wrapped around him, Alderson looked like a youthful Pancho Villa.

During the initial weeks, Wayne developed a taste for killing. His reckless style sparked a sensuous joy that was heightened by the prizes of war. He started to enjoy the heady excitement of "spraying Germans" with his machine gun. Alderson's lust was satiated as he killed scores of German soldiers in close-quarter firefights.

But Wayne was never quite able to take the killing in his stride. He was beset with severe bouts of retching when he moved closer to the mutilated bodies of the men he had just killed. His nose never adjusted to the stench of rotting corpses. The grotesque faces twisted in the mask of death could not eclipse from Alderson's mind the fact that German soldiers were people.

In the Saar-Pocket, Wayne rekindled a friendship with a buddy from home—Joe Stankowski from Canonsburg, Pennsylvania. He was in the same battallion as Wayne, but assigned to mortars. He was a burly product of the western Pennsylvania coal fields who was known by the crass nickname "Mill-hunky," and he was as kind, gentle, and likable as he was big. He was a tough soldier and everybody knew it. Joe feared for Wayne's life, and pleaded with him to get out of scouting. But Stankowski lost the argument and Alderson stayed on the point. The two stayed close friends, and Alderson, Preston, and Stankowski were inseparable.

For weeks Wayne led patrols of an advance force of Americans that swept small villages in the Saar. They took the villages systematically, moving street by street, house by house, room by room. The procedure was simple. The point man entered the house first, usually via the basement. He threw in a grenade and followed it with a burst of machine-gun spray. If Germans emerged in a posture of surrender, Wayne chose the one who appeared most fearful. The terrified prisoner would then be used as a shield for further penetration of the house. Wayne would ask the German if any of his comrades were in a room. If he said "no," Wayne pushed the prisoner into the room first, using him as a decoy. If he said "yes," the routine of alternate grenade and machine-gun spray continued until the whole building was cleared of the enemy. The same procedure was followed in the next house, and the next, until the street was secured and the village captured.

On one such expedition, the system backfired. As Wayne routinely tossed a grenade into a room, he was shocked to see it come flying back out of the door, landing at his feet. He dove for cover before the grenade detonated, vowing to refine his method to avoid such carelessness. This close brush with death awakened Alderson to his own mortality.

*MARCH 15, 1945.* The Ides of March. For the Americans contemplating full-scale invasion of Germany, the Ides were to bring a grim mixture of death and victory. "Jump-off" was scheduled for 0100. This was the day a whole army had eagerly awaited for four years. From El Alamein to Anzio, from Algiers to Normandy, the goal was the same—Germany. A strike at the heart of the enemy homeland.

The Third Division was to lead the Army into Germany. As fate decreed it, Alderson's regiment and battalion were scheduled to go first. Company B led the way. That meant that, kill or be killed, Wayne Alderson would be the first man into Germany. The official *History of the Third Infantry Division* describes the jump-off as follows:

The Division was poised on the Franco-German border, awaiting the signal for attack. It was not long coming. The date was set—March 15. The hour—0100.

In a special, last minute briefing, Iron Mike told his regimental commanders: "Within one hour after the jump-off you will be in Germany."

Events proved him right. The third infantry division reached the fringe of the long-sought goal exactly thirty-one minutes after its leading elements crossed the line of departure. The path into Germany was a thorny one. For the third push to the Rhine River also marked the

**Pfc. Wayne T. Alderson, 18.** Wayne's regiment assaulted the Siegfried Line in Germany, March 1945.

third time that the division had been assigned to a highly-fortified area and given the task of reducing all obstacles that lay in their path. The two other times were against the "iron ring" of Anzio and the "frozen crust" of the Colman Pochet . . . the ground was gummy, sticky, following recent rains.

Promptly at 0100, March 15, the first and second battalions of the seventh infantry and first and third battalions of the thirtieth infantry pushed off . . . at 0135 Company B led the third infantry division into Germany about one mile south of Utweiler. First scout Pfc. Wayne T. Alderson was the first man across.*

The point man for Company B was now on the point for the most critical maneuver of the entire Third Division. Moments before departure, the colonel in charge of the troops gave last minute instructions to Pfc. Alderson.

"Don't be afraid. We're behind you. Don't fire your weapon unless it is absolutely necessary. As soon as you fire, they'll know our position. Avoid a firefight if you possibly can."

"Point men out!"

This time Alderson was terrified. Fear paralyzed his movement. His legs were moving, pumping up and down, but he was marching in place. Wayne had to force himself to execute the most elementary dynamics of human locomotion. He willed himself to walk forward, methodically placing one foot in front of the other until his steps carried him into the night, alone.

Night patrols were always the worst. In the silent darkness, fear was accentuated and point men often experienced a sense of disorientation. Every skittering pebble sounded like an avalanche. As the pitch black swallowed him, Alderson strained to make out the silhouettes of pillboxes and foxholes. He walked quietly and carefully, trying not to stir up enemy action. He bypassed a large crater in the earth and moved on. But something about the crater worried him. Could there be a machine-gun nest concealed in it? He doubled back to check. As he approached the crater, six German soldiers sprang up. Instinctively, Wayne fired his tommy gun and threw a grenade. The

*Donald G. Taggart, ed., *History of the Third Infantry Division in World War II* (Washington, D.C.: Infantry Journal Press), 1947, pp. 328–329.

war was over for those six Germans, but the paroxysm of fire that broke the silence set the invasion of Germany in motion.

With the firefight raging, Wayne fell back to Red's position and the rest of the troops scrambled to catch up. As the column advanced, Billy Weaver stepped on a mine. He was injured, but he kept going to support his comrades.

The German machine gunners were firing effective and deadly "tracers" and "skimmers." The tracers were fired several feet off the ground, to trick the attacking Americans into thinking the guns were above their heads. Then, running upright under the tracers, the GIs would run into a volley of skimmers set waist high. Belly wounds from those bullets were one of the most feared of all injuries. A skimmer hit Billy Weaver in the stomach and he fell on the spot. This time his wound was fatal.

Out on the point, Wayne left Red and the others behind as he pushed out to penetrate the enemy. Wading across a creek, Alderson ventured alone into Germany. The German force was entrenched twenty-five feet away. Wayne hugged the ground as he waited for his company to catch up. He could hear the Germans breathing only a few yards away. He was aware of the telltale "tinny sound," a sure sign of the presence of German troops. The tinny sound was made by the rustling of canteens against the German soldiers' belts or weapons.

Behind him, Alderson heard Lt. Barber order the men to advance and back Wayne up. With that, he opened fire. A lot of men would die in that battle, but the advance line was secured.

The Americans doubled back to hit two crucial French towns from the rear. These towns had been bypassed for strategic reasons on the movement to the German border. The German soldiers occupying the towns were now cut off from their lines and exposed to a rear-guard attack. That night, both towns fell to American forces and were occupied by morning. Alderson's company took one of them, and Joe Stankowski's outfit took the other.

When dawn appeared, Wayne was back on the point. From his vantage point he witnessed a sickening sight. He could only watch helplessly as the German army executed a devastating counterattack against the town Stankowski's group had occupied. German panzer troops leveled the town and annihilated the Americans who, only hours before, had celebrated their victory. The GIs tried to surrender, but the Germans were taking no prisoners. Those who came out with their arms raised in defeat were slaughtered by German armor. Joe Stankowski was blown to bits by a direct hit from the cannon of a German tank.

When the smoke lifted and a welcome lull in fighting occurred, Wayne and Red recovered the body of Billy Weaver and brought it to an American-occupied building; Stankowski's body was irretrievable. Wayne and Red sat in the building and cried. In the short space of eight hours, their two closest friends had been killed. After they left the building, Billy's body was somehow lost and he was ultimately listed as missing-in-action. But Wayne and Red knew the truth.

Though casualties had been heavy, the overall impact of the jump-off was successful. The afternoon of March 15 was a time of rest and celebration for the Americans, but Wayne had little time for relaxation. Excited officers and news photographers descended upon him with congratulations and requests for interviews. Word had spread that Private Alderson had been the first Third Division man into Germany, thus bringing welcome recognition to the entire Seventh Regiment, a regiment weary of being mocked for their predecessors' ignominious defeat under Custer at the Little Big Horn. Wayne was escorted to the command post for pictures and interviews to be featured in the army newspaper, *Stars and Stripes.*

A high-ranking officer approached Alderson and informed him that he had been chosen to leave the front for R and R and publicity ceremonies.

Wayne said simply, "I can't go."

He desperately wanted to go and leave the battle behind him.

But after the deaths of Billy and Joe, Wayne felt he couldn't leave Red alone. Torn by feelings of guilt, and afraid of losing the respect of the other men, Wayne declined the offer.

The officer explained to the young private that the idea of leaving the line for the ceremony was not an offer but an order. Wayne protested until finally, reluctantly, the officer told him he could wait a day for his departure.

"You can stay today, but tomorrow you have to go back."

With that, the officer dismissed the photographers and writers and promised them their story the next day. But the war would break that promise within twelve hours.

The next morning Company B, led by First Scout Wayne T. Alderson, jumped off against the dreaded Siegfried Line.

The Siegfried Line was the first line of defense for the Third Reich. It was awesome. Drawing upon defense strategies proven effective in World War I, as well as more modern devices tested elsewhere in Europe and Africa, the Line was designed to make any armored assault against the interior of the Fatherland a costly one. The outer perimeter was lined with dragon's teeth, solid concrete barriers that barred the path of tanks or other armored vehicles. Backing up the dragon's teeth was a complex maze of deep trenches arranged in zig-zag fashion. The trenches were manned by German infantrymen backed up by elements of the elite 17th S. S. Panzer Division. At strategic points across the line, carefully engineered pillboxes provided a solid base of machine gun and artillery fire for those who dared to attack the line on foot. The line faced a wide expanse of open field over which any attacker must move to get to the mouth of the dragon.

Company B executed a forced march deep into a forest near the Siegfried Line. Camping in the cover near the edge of the woods, the Americans were able to look across the open field at the concrete wall that defended Germany. The foot soldiers tried to relax in the shelter of the woods as American artillery pounded the line for hours. Some of the greener troops clung to the illusion that such a shelling would actually mollify the dragon, but the veterans were wise enough to know better. When the smoke of the artillery had evaporated, the soldiers could see that the dragon's defiant grin revealed not a single visible cavity. They knew the monster could only be slain by hand-to-hand combat, and his teeth removed one at a time by manually applied explosives. That meant charging across the open field like Pickett at Gettysburg.

During the long hours of artillery bombardment, Wayne and Red were able to have a heart-to-heart talk. "This is my last day," Wayne announced grimly. "I know it. Billy didn't make it, Joe didn't make it. I'm not going to make it."

He had a premonition that this day would be his last in combat, but Alderson was not sure his omen was a fatal one. He had no intuitive certainty of death, only that this day would mark the end of combat for him. Red had a premonition as well, but it had no ambiguity: he was sure he was going to die.

As the soldiers talked into the night, the artillery stopped. An urgent fear gripped them both. They didn't pray, but Alderson did allow one pious thought to cross his mind. He made a quick vow that, if he got through the assault on the dragon, he would

Aerial photo, taken south of Zweibrücken, Germany, shows where Wayne, Red, and the men of the Third Infantry Division broke through the Siegfried Line. The path was cleared by engineers to allow armor and tanks to pass through safely several days later. March 1945.

go to church every Sunday. Wayne and Red made the custom-
ary foxhole vow to each other, that if either was killed and the
other survived, the survivor would visit the other's family after
the war.

The dawn emerged slowly, with an eerie stillness. As the sun
burned away the mist, the specter of pillboxes and dragon's
teeth filled the straining eyes of the men. It seemed as if no
artillery had ever been launched.

The hated words came soon enough: "Scouts out!"

Wayne and Red broke out of the forest in a run. The company
followed close behind. Expecting a barrage of bullets, the men
were surprised to be greeted with silence. Wayne's mind was
racing as fast as his legs as he moved far out into the clearing.
For an instant he entertained the delicious idea that the artillery had so unnerved the Germans that they had retreated,
leaving the dragon defenseless. But he knew such hopes were
idle fantasies. The Germans were there. They were waiting
. . . waiting for Wayne and the men to venture far enough into
the clearing to be at the point of no return.

The storm of battle broke with a vengeance, ushered in by an
onslaught of 88s. With the deafening sound of shelling signaling
the beginning of the firefight, the pillboxes added their staccato
beat to the fracas. Wayne was running on fear and instinct. The
rifle and machine gun fire from the trenches was so intense that
dust and metal fragments seemed to engulf him.

The sudden impact of a German bullet spun Alderson
around, but he kept running. As wetness saturated his thigh,
panicky thoughts confused him.

*I'm hit. Why don't I feel it?* He was afraid to look at what he
knew must be his own blood pouring out of his body.

But finally he chanced a peek at his thigh, as his legs churned
mechanically through the maelstrom of enemy fire. Wayne Alderson had been mortally wounded, all right—in the canteen!
He saw the shattered, jagged pieces of his canteen, and the
water soaking his pant leg. Alderson welcomed this moment of
comic relief. He wondered what the entrenched Germans

thought of this crazy American, charging their bunker and grinning like a madman.

Wayne and Red were the first to make it beyond the dragon's teeth. Firing their machine guns wildly, they jumped into the end of a trench. Some Germans who were not caught in the Americans' spray retreated toward the other end of the trench. Wayne, Red, and a handful of other GIs who made it across the field were now firmly ensconced inside the Siegfried Line. Like Jonah in the belly of the great whale, these men had been swallowed up by the dragon. But would they, like Jonah, ever be released?

Occupying one end of the German trench, the men realized they had been cut off from the main body of their battalion. Their radio had been knocked out in the firefight. They were isolated deep within the lair of the enemy. No one dared to peek over the top of the trench to monitor the progress of the rest of the company. Already German machine gunners had trained their instruments on the top of the portion of the trench occupied by this remnant of Company B. It was a standoff.

Cut off from visual and verbal contact with the company, the men were left with three options. One, they could retreat back across the open field, risking almost certain death and relinquishing the gains they had paid so dearly to achieve. Two, they could sit in their end of the trench and do nothing. This was an open invitation for the Germans in the trench with them to counterattack. Three, they could launch an attack of their own in an effort to occupy the entire trench.

Option three was chosen. The strategy was simple: conquer the trench, come out the other end; outflank the pillboxes and knock them out of commission. This would secure the trench and at the same time give the rest of the company a point of entry at the line. This option was no picnic, but it beat the other two, which offered little hope beyond total annihilation.

It was like waging war in a tunnel. Eight men started their march through the trench. Wayne was on the point, backed up by Red. Only the point man could dare fire his weapon. Red backed up Wayne with grenades. The other men, unable to fire for fear of hitting their comrades in front, were there to pick up the action if Wayne or Red should fall.

Systematically they moved down the trench, winning it yard by precious yard. Red lobbed grenades over Wayne's head, and Alderson followed up with bursts from his Thompson submachine gun. Wayne heard the tinny sound again, as the enemy retreated deeper and deeper into their private labyrinth of horror. The trench was not straight; zig-zags and spider trenches branched off the main line. Ambush could await at any turn.

The Germans were retreating too quickly; Wayne sensed the Americans were being sucked into a trap. But the GIs kept going: They had no alternative but to search out and destroy the enemy.

Without warning, Wayne found himself staring into the eyes of a German soldier. The two enemies froze like figures in a snapshot. The German was a big man, and his rifle was trained on Wayne's heart. In his other hand he held a grenade with the pin already pulled. Wayne was paralyzed with fear and confusion. *Why doesn't he shoot me?* he wondered. *What's he going to do with that grenade?*

Alderson got his answer. From ten feet, the German threw the grenade. Like an animal whose instinct is to attack and kill whatever is threatening him, Wayne disregarded the ticking time bomb at his feet and sprayed his enemy with fire. As the huge German crumpled to the ground in death, Wayne thought to himself, *What the hell did I do that for? I should be running. I'm out of time.*

He could see the grenade and knew it was too late to escape its lethal blast. Mesmerized by it, and still in the grip of paralyzing fear, Wayne watched the ugly thing explode in his face. In that frozen, timeless moment of consciousness, Wayne saw the explosion in minute detail. He saw the heat emanate from the epicenter of the hideous bomb. He watched the shrapnel flying toward his face in the unbelievable horror of slow motion.

Wayne felt as if his brain had exploded. Yet somehow he was still standing, still conscious, still alive. Stunned, numb, and disoriented, Alderson just stood there with blood gushing from his head. He was awake, but the edge of his wakefulness was being eroded by darkness. Feeling no pain, his mind swung between confusion and lucidity. He had stepped off the end of the world and was falling into a bottomless abyss.

Red rushed to Wayne's side. Disoriented, Alderson had stumbled into a position that was completely exposed to enemy fire. Embracing him in the gentlest of bear hugs and turning his back to the enemy, Red shielded his stricken friend with his own body. For this briefest of interludes, Red stood between the enemy and Wayne. Their positions were reversed. Now Red was on the point.

Red didn't speak but his eyes said to Wayne, *Don't be afraid, I won't leave you.*

But his eyes did not know the truth. Red stayed a very short time: just long enough to save a man's life and communicate the deepest and purest kind of love one man can have for another.

Red never saw the bullet coming. Death was so quick that he probably never felt it. As the bullet penetrated the back of his head, Red's blood flowed out and began to blend with Wayne's. For a second the two men stood locked in an embrace of blood and death. A stricken witness of his own destruction Wayne was vaguely aware of the clash of color going on before his eyes. Red's blood was oozing from his head, a violent stream of crimson over the orange hair. Then, quietly, Red started to sink, sliding down Wayne's body, grasping his jacket, then his belt, and finally his pant leg, until he lay dead at Alderson's feet.

Red had not run. He had done his duty beyond the limits of anyone's expectations. No one could call him a "screw-off" now.

The point man was down—dazed, bewildered, and savagely wounded. The point was no longer secure.

# 2

## To Death and Back

With Red dead at his feet, Wayne responded like a man in a dream. He reached down and groped for his helmet. His sister's photo was attached to the inner lining. As he fumbled to pick up the steel hat, he was aware that his own blood was dripping on the picture, staining it. Something snapped, and an irresistible urge to survive suddenly took hold of him. Breaking through the haze of unreality, Wayne began to scramble like a wild man.

Alderson frantically crawled, clawed, and scraped his way back along the trench. He shouted commands to himself until he turned a corner and saw his captain's ashen face. The man screamed, "What happened to you?"

At the sight of his commanding officer, Wayne suddenly felt safe. "Where are the men?" he asked.

The captain ignored his query. "Did you get the pillbox?"

When the question finally registered in Wayne's brain, he realized its import: he had failed. He had represented the hope of survival for all of them. He shouted back, "No, damn it! Don't you care what happened?"

The captain recoiled in horror at the sight of the crazed scout with the smashed skull and called for a medic.

The medic came to Alderson and administered a shot of morphine. Wayne started to crawl toward the rear of the trench, where other wounded were waiting for evacuation. the faces of the men he passed, those still unharmed, were twisted with fear. His body was lifted and passed from soldier to soldier like a bucket in a fire brigade. Almost every man whispered to him, "We'll get 'em for you. We won't take any prisoners." But Alderson could hear the hollow sound of fear ringing behind their oaths.

Pfc. Alderson reached the rear of the trench at 9 A.M. At 2 P.M. he was still there. In his confused state of semiconsciousness all he could think was, *Red's dead, Joe's dead, Billy's dead, and I'm going to die.*

Some of the wounded did die. Others were perilously close to death. At 3 P.M. the medics said, "We have to get out of here."

Abandoning hope that the few fighting men left could secure the trench and knock out the pillbox, the medics decided to evacuate the wounded back across the open field. They entertained a small hope that the enemy would honor the protocol of combat, and would not fire upon those who were clearly marked by the emblem of the Red Cross.

The medics put Wayne on a stretcher, and the litter-bearers came to carry him across the field. Alderson promptly and defiantly got off the stretcher and refused to get back on. The medics told him he was wounded too severely to walk. With head bandaged, vision blurred, and only partially coherent, Wayne refused to be carried. His refusal was not born of bravado or courage. It was born of fear. He was sure the Germans would not permit a safe evacuation, and he did not want to be an easy target on the stretcher.

As the medics with their wounded started across the field, some walking, some on stretchers, they were chopped to ribbons. From the edge of the forest, the Americans tried to supply cover fire. But most of the medics and their wounded charges were slaughtered in the open field. Feeling no pain, Wayne crawled, screamed, and stumbled his way across. He had one consuming thought: survival. Men fell all around him as he neared the tree-line. Some GIs ran out from their sylvan cover and carried Wayne to safety.

"What are you doing here, you yellow-bellied bastards? How could you stay here while we were out there alone?" In his anguish, Alderson had forgotten about the dragon's teeth. He had forgotten that the tanks were useless weapons unless the dragon was tamed.

Alderson was placed in a jeep and driven to a makeshift aid station in a nearby town. The quarters were temporary, as the Americans had not yet secured the town and sporadic fighting was still going on in the streets and houses. No sooner had they arrived at the aid station than two of Wayne's wounded comrades died. They had survived the long wait in the trench; they were two of the "lucky" survivors of the race across the clearing. Now, in the safety of medical facilities, they succumbed.

After receiving preliminary treatment at the aid station, Wayne was carried to an ambulance to be transported to a more fully equipped hospital. The ride was bumpy and dangerous, because the ambulance had to negotiate an enemy mine field. Alderson had no idea how much time elapsed as he slipped in and out of consciousness on the journey.

Finally, the ambulance stopped and Wayne found himself in an evacuation hospital somewhere in the interior of France. Along with other wounded men, Wayne was unloaded onto a floor in a big tent. People were everywhere. He was terrified.

Sometime that afternoon, Wayne Alderson reached the rim of death. No one pronounced him dead; there was no tag on his toe. But he lifted the hem of the thin veil that separates this world from what lies beyond. What happened was ineffable. Wayne felt an all-encompassing peace, calm, and joy. He was not a religious man, but he had the certain knowledge that he was in the presence of God. He couldn't see God, but he experienced His presence. "I've known the joy of marriage and of fathering a child," He says now. "I've had innumerable joys in my life. But, nothing could ever come close to what I experienced that day. Now I have less fear of dying. I'm ready to go home any time. I had a taste of heaven and now I know what grace is. I long to have the experience again. Though it happened over thirty-five years ago, I remember it as though it was in the last hour." When he felt himself leaving that beautiful presence, he fought it. He didn't want to leave, but he had to return. . . .

The theological debate about out-of-body phenomena, "death" experiences, and the like is beyond Alderson's knowledge and concern. Was his mind playing tricks on him? Was his body moving toward the final surrender of death? Was he hallucinating? Was God giving him a special glimpse into what would await him later? Was this an act of grace or the simple wish-projection of a dying man? Alderson can't answer such questions; in fact, they bore him. A simple man with strong, often stubborn convictions, Alderson clings to the memory of that precious experience.

Wayne woke up in the hospital tent, alone. Certain that he had been left behind as a corpse, he screamed. He was seized with a combination of fear and pain as the peace and joy abruptly vanished, leaving the seeds of a lifelong terror of tents.

A combat nurse appeared, the first woman to walk into Alderson's world of men. As with many of his comrades, the seeds of chauvinism had long-ago been sown into Wayne's psyche, leaving little room to value or respect women. But combat nurses had the ability to turn such men around. When the "tough" male veterans of combat were gripped by fear, they looked to these women for strength. Somehow, the nurses never seemed to panic. Their courage was often unheralded, but was not forgotten by the men they helped.

The nurse asked the wounded soldier how old he was.

"Eighteen," he mumbled.

She began to weep unashamed tears of compassion. This brutally beaten "man" in soldier's dress was just a boy. Wayne felt the warmth of her tears as they fell on his face. In this fragile moment of encounter between the souls of two human beings, Wayne began to understand that vulnerability could also be strength. This woman valued him in his brokeness.

When he left the battlefield hospital, Alderson began an odyssey of surgery and recuperation that would last for years. He had operations in Germany, France, England, and the United States to remove shrapnel and bone chips from his face and head. Five times he underwent major surgery. One such operation left him totally blind for a period of weeks. During that interlude of blackness, the world of light was gone and the terror of the night pressed upon him even while the sun was shining outside. He had to learn to eat by having the food on his plate arranged like the face of a clock. His vegetables were at three o'clock, his meat was at nine o'clock, his potatoes were at twelve o'clock. The simple act of eating had become an exhausting chore of groping for food and steering it by feel toward his mouth. He felt that everyone's eyes were on him, and tumbled deeper into a sense of humiliation. Other people could see him, but he saw no one.

Fortunately, the loss of sight was temporary. When Wayne's vision was restored he found new hope emerging for his life, and along with it a new empathy for the crippled and helpless. He felt a rush of protectiveness when he saw blind people trying to negotiate a busy intersection with their white canes. Compassion had been taken out of the realm of the abstract into the reality of action.

The period of his recuperation was a time of intense inward struggle. Apart from the physical torment of his wounds and the process of surgical repair, Wayne had to do battle with his memories. Recurring nightmares featured his buddies who were killed; he dreamed of German soldiers with their faces distorted grotesquely in death. He felt lost and alone.

The war was over and Alderson was a man without a career. Both his body and his soul were scarred by the past. Only eighteen, Wayne wasn't quite sure who he was or where he was going. Yet he had a sense of destiny that kept him functioning as he searched to discover why his friends had been killed while he had survived.

Like Jacob marked forever after wrestling with an angel, Alderson emerged from his battery of operations physically scarred. Though the surgeons skillfully rebuilt his face and head, they could not erase one indelible mark: A depression was left in the center of his forehead. To this day, the offhand remark about needing something like "a hole in the head" is not funny to Wayne Alderson. For that is exactly what Alderson looks like: a man with a hole in his head.

Surgery required that Wayne have his head shaved. Between operations he felt naked and ashamed. This was during the years when Europeans dealt with traitors and collaborators by shaving their heads in public disgrace. The bare scalp gave him an uncomfortable feeling of self-consciousness, which a Purple Heart and Bronze Star were not enough to cover. This sense of humiliation played havoc with Wayne's self-image. Here he was, still a young man; no war to fight, no hero's welcome.

During a sabbatical from the hospital, Wayne made a decision: for him, the war would not be over. Combat was all he knew, and he was good at it. He heard rumors that, incredibly, a Jewish nation was emerging out of the ashes of Auschwitz and Buchenwald. He didn't understand the subtleties of Zionism, but he was eager to return to the point. America was at peace and settling down for a prolonged period of cold war; Germany had been partitioned and the game now seemed to be played politically rather than militarily. Given these factors, Alderson decided to become a mercenary. In 1947, still in the process of surgical repair and recuperation, Wayne joined the Jewish Fighting Force that was dedicated to the liberation of Palestine and the founding of a Jewish State of Israel.

This brief venture into the Zionist movement was triggered by a visit to New York City. Two of Wayne's wartime friends who had survived the Siegfried encounter invited him to visit them in Flatbush, in the heart of Brooklyn. For six weeks Wayne visited in their homes and was "adopted" by their Jewish immigrant parents. He was an alien in their midst, and Alderson made all the mistakes a Gentile can make in a Jewish environment. He said the wrong things, wore the wrong clothes, and asked for the wrong things to eat. But his friends' parents never embarrassed him. They treated him tenderly, exercising the millennia-old tradition of honoring the stranger within their gates.

During this sojourn with the immigrants, Wayne listened to their conversations and heard their dreams of a new Palestine, of "next year in Jerusalem." He heard the stories of life in the old country, of ghettos and pogroms, of genocide and deportation. He knew what it was like to be homeless. The excitement of the conflict in the Middle East took hold of him and he made inquiries about joining the cause. Israel was the underdog, and Alderson had never been one to root for the New York Yankees.

Wayne made his way to a secret interview with a high ranking member of the Haganah who was in charge of recruiting volunteers for the Jewish cause. He was quizzed intently about his motives. He confessed that a mixture of desires had brought him to the meeting. He acknowledged that he had no skill other than combat, and warfare had become his accomplished trade. At the same time, he was haunted by fears of returning to the battlefield. The ambivalence of attraction and repulsion was at work within him. He explained that his interest in the Jewish cause had been sparked by the contagious zeal of his friends. His story satisfied the recruiting official, and Wayne signed on.

The official saw that the young Gentile intuitively understood what the Jewish cause was all about. Zionism was more than a battle over real estate. It meant the restoration of Jewish dignity —a dignity born in Yahweh's own "glory," His *kavod*. *Kavod* expressed the idea of God's weightiness, His heaviness, His own substantial value that He assigned to every person bearing His image. This was a dignity even the Holocaust could not obliterate.

Wayne was told that if he came back from the battlefield safely, his contribution to the effort would never be forgotten by the American Jewish community. The promise had the ring of truth, backed up by centuries of Jewish loyalty to friends and supporters.

A brief period of preparation and planning in New York was followed quickly by embarkation day. When the day arrived, Alderson boarded a ship at the wharf in New York. All of the passengers were American citizens bound for Tel Aviv. The cargo was contraband, as the U.S. Government had forbidden the involvement of American citizens in this foreign enterprise. Two ships were scheduled to leave port at this time. The first barely made it out of the harbor before it was intercepted by the U.S. Coast Guard. A warning was transmitted to the sister ship, still at the dock. Immediately, the men disembarked and their abortive mission was scuttled.

A further rendezvous with Jewish leaders led to the end of Alderson's career as a mercenary. Public opinion was in an uproar over American deaths in Palestine. The government became so sensitive that they began stripping any Americans involved in mercenary activities in Palestine of their citizenship. Thus Alderson was persuaded by the Jewish leaders in New York to remain at home.

Wayne had taken his citizenship for granted. Though a decorated war veteran, he was not a flag-waving jingoist. Like most Americans, he simply assumed the inviolability of his citizenship. The Jewish leaders, on the other hand, did not share his smug assumptions. They were a pilgrim people whose "citizenship" in any nation was always tenuous. Through repeated losses of citizenship they understood its value. Thus they would not permit Wayne to naively risk his birthright. Their wisdom prevailed over his brashness.

Disappointed, Alderson returned to his home in Canonsburg, Pennsylvania, near Pittsburgh, where he sought to establish himself in civilian life by working odd jobs in construction.

From a war of smoke and fire, Wayne returned home to a city

filled with the belching furnaces of steel mills built by Carnegie and Frick in the gilded age. Coal barges dotted the river as they made their way to Cincinnati, St. Louis, and down the Mississippi to New Orleans. Pittsburgh was—and still is—an ethnically mixed city where Irish, German, Italian, and Slovak immigrants met, fought, and worked their way to strength in the steel capital of the world. The time-honored drink of these men is the "boilermaker," a glass of beer and a shot of whiskey. This was Wayne's home; these were his people. More trips to the Veteran's Hospital were interspersed with a pursuit of women. After his baptism in blood, and his experience in killing and the hardness of the war, he was left with a kind of calloused aggression. He saw love as a battle, and each "victory" with a woman brought a new sense of achievement and quieted, for a moment, the feelings of uncertainty he carried in his marred body.

Halloween, 1948, changed all that. The twenty-one-year-old Alderson was still young enough to enjoy the idea of going to a Halloween party, and he and his date went to such a party at a private residence in Mt. Washington, which rises sharply from the banks of the Monongahela to provide its residents with a panoramic view of Pittsburgh's Golden Triangle.

Alderson's trip to Mt. Washington might just as well have been a trip to Mt. Olympus. Here he met his Aphrodite, who would kindle in him a new kind of love and affection for women. Her name was Nancy Holt, and her countenance betrayed her Scandinavian ancestry. Nancy appeared with an escort, but Wayne didn't take notice of the man who was next to her. Like a child transfixed by a toy store window, Alderson couldn't stop staring at this vision of loveliness. She was slender and striking in her hoop skirt costume, which was supported by the countless crinoline slips that were the rage of the late forties and early fifties. Wayne caught a glimpse of Nancy's legs, which were only partially concealed by her outfit. These were the days when Betty Grable's wartime pin-up pictures had focused men's attention on women's legs. The show business hype reached its zenith (or nadir) with the widely publicized news that Grable's gams were insured by Lloyds of London. In Nancy Holt, Wayne beheld a real-life version of Grablesque femininity.

But it was her hair that most captivated Wayne. It was long and flowing with the soft blondeness characteristic of Swedish girls. In fact, nothing about Nancy was hard. Her appearance, dress, and style all communicated tenderness and warmth. The softness of her hair suggested to Wayne demure femininity that was completely disarming to the young veteran, who was not as tough inside as he appeared outside. In short, he was awestruck by the sight of her.

Nancy noticed his stare, and their eyes met for a moment across the room. They experienced the kind of communication that takes place only in F. Scott Fitzgerald novels. It was truly an enchanted evening.

Wayne entered a state of limerance, the psychological term used to describe the popular notion of "falling in love." It is the state characterized by queasy feelings in the pit of the stomach, obsessive daydreaming, and a rebirth of adolescent excitement that sentimentalizes the ordinary and makes each encounter an exercise in romance.

Wayne left the party after he had made certain that he learned her name. He also secured her phone number from a friend. He knew this was a woman to be loved. A few days later, with the same anxiety he felt before a scouting patrol in combat, he worked up the courage to phone her. She was not home, but he left his name. Now his anxiety became sheer torment as his emotions haunted him with fears of unrequited love.

He called again. This time Nancy was home. Wayne fumbled for words, finally managing to ask Nancy for a date. When she accepted, Wayne almost jumped out of the telephone booth. It was like VJ day for him.

During the months that followed, their relationship blossomed into courtship. Wayne's feelings were inconsistent and contradictory. One day his love for Nancy made him resolved to pursue marriage; the next day his fears and insecurities made him want to flee for his life. He was unable to control her or the emotions she provoked within him.

Wayne had to return to the hospital for more medical care. The period of reconstructive surgery was over, but Alderson was still left with sporadic bouts of headaches, dizziness, and blackout spells. These residual physical problems fed internal feelings of bitterness and resentment toward the war. Wayne's spirit was not yet settled. But what the doctors could not cure, Nancy began to heal.

She visited the hospital almost daily. She brought a quality of tenderness that Wayne needed sorely. Their combined portrait showed a profile of opposites. Normally brash, aggressive, and outspoken, Wayne had to deal with a woman of quiet demeanor who was disciplined and committed to traditional values. Her gentle spirit, however, could be misleading. Beneath her genteel appearance was a woman with strength that resisted manipulation. She knew how to handle Wayne. Where Wayne was wild, Nancy was controlled; where he was abrasive, she was smooth; where he was confused, she was lucid. Weaknesses met strengths, collided, and merged.

This was a time of deep personal struggle for Wayne. Though he was not given to moods of protracted depression or melancholy, his life was not characterized by happiness. By contrast, Nancy was a joyous person, with a kind of happiness that was infectious. She introduced a new dimension into Wayne's world.

Nancy was also a woman of deep religious faith. She lived by the conviction that her life was covered by the umbrella of God's wise providence. The "will of God" was not a fatalistic omen or smug religious formula for her. She believed in a personal God whose will touched the mundane affairs of men and women. She viewed the events of her life, including meeting Wayne Alderson, as a real part of God's eternal plan. Like the Biblical Deborah, she looked to heaven when earth gave no answers.

This was all somewhat foreign to Wayne, but he wasn't particularly interested in why this woman was what she was. He simply accepted her at face value, knowing he could not live without her. Nancy Holt was the product of old-world family rearing. Her father, Emil Holt, emigrated from Sweden and secured employment as a boilermaker in the roundhouse of the Pennsylvania Railroad in Pittsburgh. He met his bride, Ellen, while on shipboard to America. The Holts had two children, Nancy and Carl. Carl became a career officer in the U.S. Air Force, flying many missions of the type which antedated the notorious U-2 incident featuring Francis Gary Powers.

Emil Holt was a man of simple pleasures. Nicknamed "Swede," he took his delight in music. His instruments were the accordian and harmonica; his favorite dance, the polka. He was both tough and gentle. Noted for his kindness, he had a special enthusiasm for people. During Wayne and Nancy's courtship days, Emil warmly welcomed Wayne into his home, convinced his name was "Anderson." Emil didn't realize that Wayne wasn't a Swede until after Wayne and Nancy were married.

Ellen Holt ranks as one of the most influential people in Wayne Alderson's life. He calls her "the kindest person I ever met." She was the matriarch of the Holt family. During the courtship period, Ellen worried about Wayne's ability to settle down and engage in meaningful employment that would provide a stable home. She wondered if a man addicted to combat could become a gentle father to his children. Her posture toward Wayne was not one of critical resistance, but of encouragement. She spoke to him of going to school, of earning a college degree. When Mrs. Holt spoke, Wayne listened intently, impressed by her sincerity. She became his confidante; not merely a mother-in-law, but one of his closest friends. He went to her with his problems and his joys. The atmosphere of the Holt house was a marked contrast to Wayne's memories of his own family background. Here were no violent explosions of anger, or vehement words of argument. The strongest passion of conflict Wayne ever witnessed there was in words like, "Oh,

Nancy" or "Oh, Mother." Wayne wanted very much to be a member of a household like that.

Alderson was born in Canonsburg, Pennsylvania, the town that spawned the world's most famous barber, Perry Como. It was also the cradle of the Polish crooner, Bobby Vinton. Lank Alderson, Wayne's father, was not so famous. He was a coal miner, the son of a coal miner, indeed the fourth generation of coal miners. He spent his life deep in the Pennsylvania coal mines. Every day he dug in the pits far beneath the surface of the earth. He fathered seven children, four boys and three girls. Wayne was right in the middle.

The Aldersons lived in company housing and did their shopping at the company store, romanticized in Tennessee Ernie Ford's popular ballad *Sixteen Tons*. But there was nothing romantic about the system. It didn't take long for many struggling miners to "owe their souls to the company store." The amount on many paychecks was "o," which meant that the entire wage went to pay off debts amassed at the company store.

As a boy, Wayne was aware that his father lived most of his life in darkness. The men left for the mines at 4 A.M., and returned to their homes after sunset. Their days were spent laboring in the darkness of the mines, illuminated only by artificial light. As the men returned from the mines they were heard before they were seen, and it was at home that Wayne first heard the tinny sound that served him so well in Germany. In this case, the sound was produced by the clatter of metal lunch boxes as the men made their way to and from the mines.

Wayne's father and the other miners enjoyed some vulgar forms of entertainment. Way beyond the prowess of tobacco-juice spitters were the exploits of his father and his friends in coal-dust blowing contests. The men competed in distance and accuracy games to see who was most adept in expelling the accumulation of a day's worth of coal dust from their nostrils. The quantity of soot was a visible measure of a miner's worth.

Lank Alderson was one of the best. The more coal dust he accumulated in his nostrils, the harder he had worked that day. A nose full of coal was a "black badge of courage."

Wayne's childhood was a time of turmoil and violence in the coal fields. The men had organized a union with the help of John L. Lewis and Phillip Murray, and the company was determined to break it up. They hired mounted "coal and iron police" to make sure there were no attempts at union organizing. They terrified young Wayne. Their billy clubs were fierce and effective weapons, and a miner's status was often measured by the number and size of the scars on his head left by the police. They rode their horses into the middle of crowds, and on some occasions up the front steps and into the living rooms of people's homes. These methods of force and violence left a lasting impression on Lank Alderson's son.

Danger and suffering were daily occurrences in the mines. Wayne recalled the day his uncle was caught in a slate fall. He was pinned beneath hundreds of pounds of slate, trapped under the earth. His cries brought Lank to his side. Acting with the superhuman strength that often comes to people in crisis situations, Lank pulled his brother to safety just as the mine roof caved in.

Later, a similar mine accident brought disaster and humiliation to the Alderson household. Lank suffered a compound fracture of the leg in a slate fall, and the injury made it impossible for him to go down into the pit. His career as a miner was finished. As a matter of course, the Alderson family was evicted from company housing. What Harold Robbins fictionalized in *Memories of Another Day,* the Aldersons experienced in real life.

Lank had married Edith Rathbone as a beautiful young bride of sixteen. She was no stranger to the coal fields, her father and brothers all worked in the mines. It was natural that she would marry a miner. But bearing and raising seven children in this cold, dark world put strains on her and on the marriage. When the Aldersons were evicted, Lank, broken and defeated, left the family.

With no man and no money, their options were grim. Welfare officials urged Edith to give up her children and place them in a county home, but she could not bear to lose them. She determined, in resolute Alderson fashion, to find a way to keep the family together. With tears of frustration, Edith led her children to a nearby ball field and promptly set up a tent to serve as a new dwelling place for her family.

For the Alderson children, the exile from company house to boy scout tent was the nadir of familial disgrace. For the rest of their lives, each would bear scars from the experience.

Edith Alderson found a level piece of ground at the base of a slope on a remote corner of a large vacant lot used by neighborhood children for a baseball diamond. Afforded some shelter by trees bordering a creekbed, the tent was set up with twine pulled taut by pegs driven into the clay. The running water of the stream would serve adequately as a water supply for drinking, cooking and bathing. There was no electricity, of course, and the tent was illumined at night by kerosene-fueled miner's lamps. There was no stove, no furnace, no plumbing, no toilet. There was barely room in the small canvas shelter for two army cots.

The youngest child, a small baby, went to stay temporarily with its grandmother. At night, the two cots were shared by the children—the three girls huddled together in one cot while the boys shared the other. Wayne was given the bottom half of one cot while his brothers shared the top. Sleep was difficult for all the children as they struggled for comfortable positions with feet in each other's faces. Edith worked nights at a bar, and slept during the day.

Five factors made life in the tent miserable for the children. The first was most basic—fear of the dark. Night sounds were magnified in the dark tent, and trees cast eerie shadows on walls. The children felt totally exposed within the canvas flaps which offered little protection from the world outside.

The second factor was the constant assault of noise. Just across the creek was the main branch of railroad tracks that serviced the area mines. At all hours of the night freight trains pulling long chains of coal cars roared past the tent, shaking the ground and causing the flimsy cots to vibrate. Wayne's older sister Lil is still tormented with recurring nightmares of menacing trains.

"I can still hear them in my sleep. 'Clickety-clack, clickety-clack,' and then the shrill whistle that made us want to scream." But they weren't allowed to cry; their mother told them to be brave.

The third torment was the unrelenting dampness. Though the hillside provided a buffer from the wind, it had an opposite effect on drainage. As moisture flowed naturally toward the stream, it had no respect for the human structure in its path. The perpetual dampness made for mud and mildew and was augmented by the fourth factor, coldness.

It was summer, and one would think coldness would not be a hardship. Other children delighted in the opportunity to sleep out at night, and suburban families were beginning to take interest in summer camping. But the Aldersons weren't camping out—this was their home and the thrill of living outside was quickly diminished by damp bed clothes that left them constantly chilled.

But the elements of nature that made survival in summer difficult and impossible in the winter, were minor compared to the pain of public humiliation. The tent house became an object of scorn for the other children in the community. At night they came *en masse* and played cowboy and Indian games. Pretending the Alderson tent was a teepee, the youths whooped and hollered around it. They threw rocks at the tent and slashed it with knives. The Aldersons suffered their shame and public humiliation in silence, huddled together inside, seeking warmth and protection. The children were terror-stricken as they watched the darting shadows of their tormentors on the canvas walls. They cringed when bottles hit the roof and sides and broke, saturating their thin veil of protection.

Perhaps the worst torment was the singleness of their shame. As they peered out of the tent flaps at night, they did not behold countless other families sharing their desperate situation. Instead, they could see houses on the distant hills of Canonsburg, aglow with electric lights, adorned with curtains in the windows and cars in the driveway. It was like looking at another world, a world of warmth and security that was tantalizingly beyond their grasp. They felt like freaks, alone and desperate.

As winter approached, Edith knew her children could not continue to survive in the tent. She applied for assistance, going on relief, an ignominy that tried her tough spirit, but one she endured in order to keep the children together.

The tent was abandoned, but the hurt lingered on. Wayne was never able to erase the experience from his mind. He is still morbidly phobic about tents, and his wartime awakening in a field hospital tent was as terrifying as the war itself.

During the day, Nancy worked in the training department of the J & L Steel Corporation. Her weekends were usually filled with church work, and she was a devoted teacher in the Sunday school. So courtship had to be squeezed into busy schedules that offered them little time to be alone. Their consolation came courtesy of the Duquesne Incline, the antiquated cable car that runs ascending and descending routes from Mt. Washington to the South Side Railroad Station of Pittsburgh. It was ironic—even symbolic—that Wayne and Nancy sought the safety of the incline as an inexpensive and relatively private trysting place. They would ride the incline, first up, then down, then back up again. Perhaps this was Nancy's best preparation for marriage to Wayne.

The courtship lasted five years. Nancy was open to marriage, but Wayne was still unsettled. Haunted by memories of war, he hesitated about making final commitments. He didn't trust his own promises. He had failed to keep one very important promise—his pact with Red. Wayne had never visited Red's family, as he said he would. He was afraid of meeting Red's parents, convinced that his presence would only stir new anguish for them. *Better to let the past alone,* he thought. Guilt plagued him for another reason. He felt personally responsible for Red's death.

Wayne spoke to Nancy often of these things. Finally, she

prevailed upon him to keep his vow. In 1950, five years after Red was killed, Wayne made his journey by bus to Derry, New Hampshire. There he met Red's parents and brother and sisters. Wayne arrived filled with anxiety, but he was immediately put at ease. The Preston family welcomed him almost as if he were Red himself. He was treated as a family member, even given Red's room as his lodging place. His visit lasted nearly a week. The family was deeply touched by Wayne's account of Red's sacrificial heroism. Red's parents spoke with pain about the fact that their son's body was never returned home. He was buried at St. Avold. Wayne made a new promise, this time to Red's family, that someday he would visit Red's gravesite in France.

His debt to Red was paid, the vow finally fulfilled. The weight that had burdened him was lifted, freeing him to leave the Prestons and return to Pittsburgh.

Wayne and Nancy were married in 1953, in a small church on Mt. Washington. Soon after their honeymoon, they purchased a home in the nearby suburban community of Pleasant Hills, which was equidistant from Mt. Washington and Wayne's family home in Canonsburg.

As they settled into the new community, Wayne took two big steps that would help to shape the family's destiny. First, he began college. For Wayne, this meant a five-year trek to night school at Robert Morris College in Pittsburgh, where he studied accounting and business administration. Here he acquired the tools that ultimately helped him reach the upper echelons of industrial management. Second, acquiescing to Nancy's wishes, he joined the church—at last fulfilling his other foxhole vow.

Church was a new experience for Wayne. The Pleasant Hills Community Church was unusual. Though affiliated with the United Presbyterian denomination, it welcomed people from a wide variety of religious and non-religious backgrounds. It was truely a "community" church, built under the leadership of Dr. Paul Franklin Hudson. Other churches could be found in Pleasant Hills, but the religious life of the town was dominated by the community church. About twenty-five hundred members graced its rolls, and made the church a pivotal center for community activities. Though still not a "religious" man, Wayne joined into these activities with enthusiasm. In due time, he was elected a deacon, and later an elder.

Alderson's involvement inclined to youth projects, which led him into a ten-year tenure as a Little League coach. In 1956, Wayne took on the added responsibility of coaching the church basketball team, which played in a city-wide league organized by the YMCA. The Pleasant Hills team soon took on the style and the personality of their coach—they literally fought their way to a play-off game for the championship of Pittsburgh, their games were marked by fierce competition that more than once erupted in brawls. No one watching would have guessed this was a church-sponsored team.

The city championship was a big event. The opposing team, a finely tuned squad of twenty players, appeared on the court in dazzling warm-up suits. Their entrance was awesome and their size intimidating. Wayne's boys numbered a total of eight players, including two substitutes who rarely played. No warm-up suits for this small group of boys, who resembled warriors more than basketball players. The game is still savored with sweetness by Alderson. He relishes the recollection of his boys running the opposition into the ground and carrying off the trophy. He remembers Sonny, a tough little guard, stealing the ball and dribbling the length of the court to score while his teammate put a bone-crushing body block on a defender, which somehow was not noticed by the referee. A group photo of the team, featured in a local newspaper, graces the wall of Alderson's office today.

As the Aldersons settled into the suburbs, Wayne gradually began to scale the management ladder. In 1965, Wayne accepted a job in the financial department of Pittron Steel, a steel foundry in Glassport, Pennsylvania. That year, an unexpected occurrence disrupted forever the course of his life. The God who spared that life was now calling in his marker.

Wayne's "call" came in the middle of the night. He had a dream. It was not one of the disturbing nightmares that had troubled Wayne's sleep in the years following the war. This dream had a different kind of intensity and was vividly real. He was startled awake at 4 A.M., as a Bible verse was forcibly impressed on his mind like a steer with a brand burned into its hide. The words of the text were not given, but chapter and verse appeared as numbers on an illuminated digital clock: Matthew 10:32.

Wayne woke up in a cold sweat, suffering the awesome dread that often attends a close encounter with the Holy. He awakened Nancy by exclaiming, "God spoke to me, God spoke to me!"

Nancy—the religious member of the household—responded, "You're dreaming, go back to sleep!" But Wayne persisted until Nancy asked, "All right, what did God say?"

"Matthew 10:32," Wayne replied. "Get me a Bible. I want to know what it says."

Alderson was not a diligent student of sacred scripture; indeed, he didn't even qualify as a novice. For him the Bible was the "Church's book." He was familiar enough with passages that every American hears on numerous occasions, but he had never read the book himself. He didn't even know if there *was* a Matthew 10:32. To Wayne, the Bible was only a symbol; like the cross, it served as one of the trappings of the life of the church. He knew it was supposed to be holy, but he didn't know why. Its content was a mystery to him, a jumble of "begats and all that stuff," with no apparent practical application.

With feverish interest, Wayne joined Nancy in a nocturnal search for the content of Matthew 10:32. They found it. The words read simply, "Whoever shall confess me before men, him will I confess also before my Father which is in heaven."

Wayne trembled at the words, and read the next verse, Matthew 10:33. The words struck like lightening: "But whoever shall deny me, him will I also deny before my Father which is in heaven."

This verse carried an ominous threat. Wayne mused, *Why did God give me Matthew 10:32 rather than 10:33? I received the promise rather than the threat.*

This was Alderson's second encounter with God, forcing him to recall his field hospital experience on the rim of death. It was not a "Damascus Road" experience, which would instantly transform him into a valorous saint. But real changes began to take shape within him. He started to become a "true believer," with a single-minded vision. Such men are viewed by some as dynamic and by others as stubborn, by some as visionary, by others as a monomaniacal. His vision was focused on one thing —the work world. That is where God had to be if He was anywhere. With a zealot's desire, he resolved either to find God there, or bring Him there.

In his midnight vision of Matthew 10:32, Wayne Alderson got a giant hint as to why God had allowed him to return from death. This was the missing piece of the puzzle. Religious faith passed beyond his superficial involvement in the Church. The name of Jesus would no longer be a word that passed over his lips as an undeleted expletive. For the first time, his faith was being fleshed out into a personal mission.

# 3

## Strike

It was a long way from the Siegfried Line to the picket line, but Wayne Alderson made the journey step by step. He made good use of his college degree and industrial experience, and by 1969 he had worked his way up to controller and chief financial officer at Pittron. As controller, Wayne was responsible for the financial management of the company, filling the role of a pencil man. It didn't take a financial wizard to see that Pittron was in trouble. The foundry had the working conditions of a coal mine, for Pittron's employees it was a place of labor unrest and racial hatred.

One of many steel mills that punctuate the topography of the "steel valley" of western Pennsylvania, the foundry was massive, covering seven blocks along the banks of the Monongahela on the edge of Glassport. Inside, the foundry vibrated with a cacophony of sounds. Sirens wailed as overhead cranes traveled back and forth across the plant. The dissonant sounds of clanging hammers, rolling cars, and riveting machines bombarded the ears and wracked the nerves. The acrid aroma of sulfur mixed with odors of grease and soot was noxious—there was no escaping the oppressive smell that hung in the plant day and night.

The steel foundry was not a pretty place. No stainless steel rollers, no polished brass or aluminum brightened the facilities. A steel foundry cannot function without creating perpetual grime, and decades of collected dirt defied the strongest detergents. The foundry walls were lined with windows at the top— at least they resembled windows in size and form. But windows are designed to provide light. Covered by a film of brown and yellow soot, these windows were almost opaque. What light filtered through cast an eerie glow of twilight in the mill, which seemed to operate on the edge of darkness.

The floor of the foundry was strewn with the refuse of men who weren't concerned with beauty. Discarded soup cups, candy and cigarette wrappers, and a plethora of litter made the foundry look like a baseball stadium after the fans have gone home and before the maintenance crew has tidied up. Pittron was a filthy place to work. It did not bring out the best in its men.

*OCTOBER 1972.* The decade of the sixties was over. Social upheaval, characterized by the civil rights movement, Vietnam, and Berkeley's Free Speech Movement had all but disappeared. The public was sick of radicalism. The early seventies witnessed a subtle shift in the arena of protest movements. From the streets and campuses, the outcry moved to the factories and office buildings. The new wave of protest centered on issues of dignity in the work world. At the forefront of the movement was the feminist cause. Women picketed not only for equal pay and job opportunities, but for equal dignity, respect, and value as human beings.

The Women's Movement helped raise the public's consciousness of non-economic issues. These issues of dignity found fertile ground in the work world. Symbolic of the transition was the experience of the Lordstown strike. Commenting on the significance of Lordstown—the General Motors complex that

had the most automated auto assembly line in the world—
*Pittsburgh Post Gazette* staff writer Peter Leo said:

Pundits and academics saw the strike as the Woodstock of the industrial world, a critical turning point in our social evolution. We had been
used to rebellious long-haired students on the one side and contented
middle Americans on the other. Now things were blowing up in middle America. . . . The strike at Lordstown represented nothing less than
a generation's rebellion against union and management, a collision
between the traditional union goals of decent income and job security
and the yearnings of the young for more than mindless labor.*

Lordstown was not an isolated incident. It merely served to
highlight what was taking place in the work world nationally.
The burning of draft cards and brassieres was giving way to
sophisticated industrial sabotage. The work force was angry and
bent on revenge. In 1973, for the first time in nationwide bargaining history, UAW negotiations focused on working conditions rather than wage demands.

If Lordstown's frustrations were great, Pittron's were even
greater. Lordstown settled its strike in twenty-one days. Pittron's lasted four times as long.

In 1972, Pittron was on the verge of explosion. So much hostility churned between labor and management that tension was
at a peak. The situation, once a guarded truce, had become a
cold war on the brink of eruption. On the surface, the issues at
Pittron appeared to be economic. The union contract had ex-
pired in 1971 and, because of the severe financial plight of the
company, the union leaders had agreed to a one-year extension
of the current contract. This meant, of course, a temporary
freezing of all worker benefits. It was agreed that the new
contract would take into consideration the benefits that were
postponed. But when the extension was up, the union alleged
that management had reneged on the promise of making up
lost benefits. The workers felt betrayed by the company and
their anger increased.

*19 March 1979, p. 1.

Beneath the surface of their anger, the workers were feeling animosity over other issues, qualitative issues concerning matters of dignity and personal respect that were difficult to resolve at a bargaining table. Hear their comments:

"Many times when I came in here I wanted to punch a foreman in the mouth or call him a son of a bitch. . . . Best a black man could do was chipping. Make a long story short—all the dirty work. . . . It was a drab and dreary place—all that sand and rubble. . . . In addition to the union people, management people were bastards. . . . We were considered second class citizens. . . . If you had a little grievance and wanted to talk it out, they would tell you 'no' before you even opened your mouth. . . . I was considered a bum. They made me that way. . . . It was a jungle. . . . You walked past the boss. He didn't care if he talked to you or not. Drop his head. You were nothing. . . . I never had one year of steady work. . . . The work was hard but a man don't mind working if people speak to you right. . . . If things didn't change, we were going to burn this place down. . . . Some of us workers here, we have given this company most of our lives. . . . I am an unhappy man. My family is unhappy. Life just isn't the same."

On October 26, 1972, the men struck. Led by the hardboiled, fire-breathing United Steel Workers Local 1306 president, Sam Piccolo, the union shut down the plant. For eighty-four days the only fires at Pittron were those burning in steel drums outside the gates, where striking pickets tried vainly to keep warm. Through the winter months the plant was idle.

Alderson remembers the strike vividly. It was particularly bitter, characterized by charges and countercharges. He called it "eighty-four days of hell."

"I saw men outside, standing around the drum fires and huddling near a makeshift shed. I thought about their families. It was Christmas. The strike meant no paycheck. It meant few, if any, presents for the children. It meant at least a year of economic recovery for the workers before their new pay increases would catch up with their losses from the walkout. It all seemed so unnecessary, so useless. But I was convinced they weren't wrong. If I were a union man under those conditions, I would have closed the plant down. I would have struck."

But Wayne wasn't a union man. He belonged to the ranks of management, and had been involved in management's frantic efforts to avert such a costly strike. The strike was not a precipitous action born of the moment; it had been months in coming.

Over the previous three years, Pittron's financial condition had deteriorated badly. During that time, the operation showed a loss of nearly six million dollars. The company was at the breaking point and could ill afford a lengthy shutdown.

Shortly before the strike, a major purge decimated the ranks of top management. Several top-level executives were "retired." Few survived with their jobs intact. One of the survivors was Wayne Alderson.

Wayne had recently attended an advanced management course co-sponsored by Harvard University and Textron, Pittron's parent company. He caught the attention of Textron's board chairman, G. William Miller (who was later to become chairman of the Federal Reserve Board, and then Secretary of the Treasury). Alderson had been outspoken in questioning current management operations and methodology. He argued that the technique of "management by confrontation"—intimidation of workers by management—did not work. The company had shown losses for thirty consecutive months. Confrontation merely served to destroy labor morale, which inevitably brought lower production, poor quality workmanship, and a high rate of absenteeism.

After the shake-up, Miller had appointed a new president of Pittron. Wayne Alderson was now elevated from controller to vice-president in charge of operations. Miller thrust the expendable Alderson, once again, onto the point. These changes were made just before the strike, and it was arguable whether or not there would be any operations left to manage. The strike was virtually a *fait accompli,* but it was hoped that the new leadership in management would settle the strike quickly and turn the plant around once the strike was over.

Only days after the purge, the men "hit the bricks" and the strike was on. Labor's attitude was one of hostility and mistrust. They were convinced the company had lied to them and had cheated them out of their benefits. Under their demands seethed a deep hatred and resentment toward management. The workers wanted to "get even" even if it meant hurting their own cause. The strike provided the men with an opportunity to fight back and hurt the company legally.

Management was equally bitter, fearing the strike would put the company out of business. Management was convinced that it could not aquiesce to the demands of the union. Given Pittron's precarious financial status, the union's demands might tip the scales toward liquidation. Some executives were concerned that, with increasing powers of unions and the restrictions they imposed, management was rapidly losing its right to manage. With rising inflation and lowering rates of productivity, the matter of efficiency became paramount. Union restraints did not allow management a free hand in establishing efficient operations. Thus it was a classic standoff, both sides firmly entrenched and unwilling to yield anything in the negotiations.

With negotiations paralyzed, the strike dragged on through Thanksgiving and Christmas. The longer the strike continued, the more bitter it became. Chickens replaced turkeys on Thanksgiving tables, and the muted Christmas served to deepen the resentment on both sides.

To make things worse, Pittron's customers began to get uneasy as early signs of corporate panic began to show. Orders were canceled and customers sought ways to protect their vested interests, which were locked up behind Pittron's gates. They wanted to remove products which were being held captive in the plant.

Some customers tried to move their trucks through the gates, which meant crossing the picket line. Violence erupted instantly when Piccolo and his men tried to stop the drivers. One trucker rammed his vehicle through the iron gate. With that move, the mass of enraged picketers erected a barricade to prevent the truck from leaving. As the ranks of strikers swelled into an angry mob, the police arrived. The strikers engaged the police in a shouting and shoving match, but order was quickly restored. The trucker escaped during the melee, but without his truck. This incident made Piccolo a hero to his men. But as the strike dragged on and negotiations bogged down, the men began to question Piccolo as well as management.

In mid-December, Pittron's new president and Alderson went to Providence, Rhode Island, to visit G. William Miller. Their task was to present their financial and operating plan for the new year. In addition to plans for 1973, the two men presented their board chairman with a master plan for five years. But Miller's primary concern was the strike. Unless that was settled, the five-year plan would be purely academic.

"When will the strike end?" he asked them. Will it be soon?"

They couldn't answer the questions. They had no idea when the strike would end. Their uncertainty showed, and Miller was less than impressed with the new master plan. He said finally, "How will this plan ever work? I don't think you can make it."

Rashly, Wayne responded, "Give us a chance. Judge us by results. Look at the bottom line. If we don't meet the plan, fire us."

Miller was surprised by Wayne's challenge. He was not accustomed to his officers speaking to him like this. He hesitated, then replied, "Fair enough." The meeting was over.

On the elevator, Pittron's president turned to Wayne and said,

"You know we can't make the plan work."

But Alderson was determined to make the plan work. The plan had to work, not only for the company's sake but for the sake of the men and their families. He pulled out all stops to make it go. He met daily with his management team, preparing for the end of the strike. Wayne conceived a bold and innovative operation to earn the workers' trust and to encourage them to pull together for better quality, better production and better morale. The plan was called Operation Turnaround.

It focused on effectiveness rather than efficiency. Wayne knew the difference between efficiency and effectiveness. Simply stated, he defined efficiency as "doing things right" and effectiveness as "doing the right things." He understood that doing things right was not very helpful if the things you were doing were not the right things. He wanted to do the right things first, and then worry about being more efficient. He was convinced that management by confrontation was ineffective. The methods might be honed and polished, but all they achieved was efficient destruction. Wayne was challenging sacred assumptions of traditional management techniques.

The other managers listened. Some were scornful and ridiculed Wayne's ideas. But his enthusiasm was contagious, and soon most of them began to follow Wayne's leadership as he ventured out to Pittron's point.

While preparations for Operation Turnaround were being made and the strike negotiations remained at a stalemate, God tapped Alderson on the shoulder for the third time. A group of friends from the church persuaded him to go on a weekend retreat held at a facility tucked away in a remote section of the mountains of western Pennsylvania. Wayne expected the retreat to offer him a brief respite from the daily strain of worrying about Pittron's future. He anticipated a time of relaxation and refreshment before he had to return to the corporate wars.

He did not relax. Instead, his conscience was stung by the remarks of the weekend speaker. The theme was a challenge to churchmen to put their faith and values to the test in the real world. They were told to come out from under the shelter of their steeples and into the marketplace.

The speaker likened the Church in an age of secularism to an Indian reservation. Intrusions of God were not welcome in the public sector. Believers could be "safe" only if they stayed on the "reservation." He challenged the idea that separation of Church and State meant the same thing as separation of State and God. He maintained that God's authority applied to all of His creation, and His values were to be applied to all of life.

Civil institutions should not become churches, but they were still fully accountable to God.

Wayne remembered the midnight encounter he experienced years before. In the speaker's address, Wayne heard God saying to him, *Come off the reservation . . . confess me before men.*

Returning to work, Wayne discovered that rumors of Pittron's closing were fast circulating throughout the steel valley. Management was divided on the question, but strong recommendations were being made that the plant be closed immediately. Operation Turnaround was beginning to be viewed as "Alderson's Folly," an idiot's fantasy. Time was running out.

With this crisis looming, Alderson had a private meeting in his home with Francis "Lefty" Scumaci, then a staff representative of the International Steel Worker's Union. The meeting was risky business because Wayne was not part of the official negotiating team appointed by Pittron.

Lefty trusted Wayne. He knew Wayne was "management," but he also understood Wayne's background. He knew Alderson had come from a family background of poverty and suffering. His roots were in labor though his job was in management. In a sense, Alderson's family background provided him with a bridge to communicate with the worker. Wayne and Lefty spoke late into the night about Alderson's childhood in the coal fields of Western Pennsylvania.

Lefty was convinced that Wayne understood the rank and file. Their lengthy discussion ended with a promise by Scumaci. "I'll try to set up a meeting with Abel. He's in Washington, but I'll contact him as soon as possible."

The next day Scumaci got through to I. W. Abel, the international president of the United Steel Workers of America, and set up the meeting. This meeting laid the initial groundwork for settling the strike.

In the meantime, Alderson sought to stay out of any direct negotiations, keenly aware that he was not a member of the Pittron negotiating team. But over that January weekend, he was forced to get involved. A call was put through to the Pleasant Hills Church, where Alderson was in a meeting. The message was simple: "Piccolo wants to meet you. Now."

Sam Piccolo was the scourge of management, its perennial thorn in the flesh. Management men always had enough sense to give Piccolo a wide berth. No one wanted to deal with him, least of all Alderson. The two men knew each other vaguely, kept apart by the invisible wall between labor and management. They were wary adversaries, each keeping an appropriate distance from the other. Though their family backgrounds were similar, their present circumstances were radically different.

Sam Piccolo was born and raised in Curry, Pennsylvania. Curry is a socioeconomic anomaly. Curry is a town one would expect to find somewhere along the banks of the Monongahela, but it is not a mill town. It is a landlocked "inner city" situated in the middle of one of Pittsburgh's most affluent areas. The South Hills area of Pittsburgh is synonymous with suburbia. Such communities as Mt. Lebanon, Upper St. Clair, Bethel Park, Whitehall, Pleasant Hills, and Greentree comprise this mecca of the middle class. It is the residential area of management, not labor. Yet right in the center of the South Hills is the small, insular town of Curry, bordering an even smaller black ghetto known as Horning.

Surrounded by parks, Curry exists in a small valley, which hides its broken-down ugliness from its more prosperous neighbors. In the old days Curry was a nerve center of coal mining. Deep mines penetrated the earth far beneath the surrounding hills.

The coal mining operations of Curry are no more. It is almost a ghost town, with a few old buildings from another era giving mute testimony to the town's former significance. The descendants of the original miners who remain in the valley go elsewhere to find employment.

Curry also produced Ned Barberich, the "big bear" of Curry. His slavic bulk is enough to intimidate the meanest of men. Ned is a shoemaker. Sandwiched in a crevice between two white collar businesses, Ned has been plying his trade for over thirty years. His shop gives meaning to the expression, "hole in the wall." It is a perfect pie-shaped building wedged between the other two with its widest point no more than ten feet across. There the customers congregate to present Ned with their worn and dilapidated footwear. Behind the counter Ned stands quietly smiling, speaking few words as he goes through the daily exercise of the cobbler. His work area is never more than four feet wide. He is barely able to move without bumping into the grinding and cutting machines of his trade. For three decades he has stood in that shop serving as an ambassador from the old world to the new.

These were the kind of men who came out of Curry. Big men. Hard men. Men with a warm spot for people. Men with romantic ideals that were never dispeled by the sophistication of progress. That is the breed of man Sam Piccolo belongs with.

Sam Piccolo was born in 1935, the child of Italian immigrants. The Piccolos were proud people willing to pay the price of hard labor to maintain their dignity and independence. This is the family that produced Sam's more famous distant cousin Brian, the tragic hero of *Brian's Song*.

Sam's father began his career in America by working in the coal fields. In those days, mules were used as beasts of burden —better a dead mule than a dead miner. In some respects, the mules were more valuable to the coal operation than Bill Piccolo. He was shrewd enough to understand the importance of the mules to his own job security, he trained them to respond to commands given in Italian. Since the mules didn't understand English, Bill was always needed to give them instruction.

After a few years of mining, the senior Piccolo, who had fathered seven children, saved enough money to open his own barber shop in Curry. Since money was scarce, many of Bill's customers paid for his tonsorial services with vegetables, home baked pies, and an occasional chicken. Thus the Piccolo's, though not well paid, were usually well fed.

But when Sam reached the ninth grade, economic difficulties

hit the household and he was called upon to carry his share of the family burden. He quit school and went to work hauling ashes. The wages he earned from this job were turned over to his father. The decision to leave school was difficult for Sam, not because of any great interest in scholarship but because Snowden Township High School offered him an excellent opportunity to develop his athletic skills. The football coach drooled at the prospect of Sam's returning to school. He interceded with the administrative officials to allow Sam to return. But the administration had serious reservations about allowing him back in. Sam was big, he'd had a taste of the adult world, and he was considered wise beyond his years. They feared that Sam had made an adjustment to the world of adults, and his return as a man among boys would be unsettling to the high school kids. The administration decided it would be best not to allow Piccolo to come back.

Sam was hurt by the school's decision. He felt sentenced to a life of hauling ashes. He stuck it out with the ash company, and hooked up with an amateur soccer team to have an outlet for his athletic aspirations. He was a natural soccer player who rapidly developed into a bona fide star. Sam's agility, coupled with bold, aggressive play, caught the eye of the coaches and he was selected as a fullback for the District All Stars. From his all star competition, Piccolo was given a tryout for the Pan American Games. He was selected as an alternate for the finals in New York. The coaches at Snowden High School cried all the way to the football stadium.

Sam's success in sports was short-lived. A hitch in the Army interrupted his career and put his life on a different course. In 1956, Piccolo, twenty-one years old, joined the infantry. The Army trained him in various skills and afforded him the opportunity to gain his high school diploma. He moved from Morse Code Operator to Radio Chief. He liked the military and resolved to be a good soldier. For seventeen straight months Sam was chosen "Soldier of the Month," shattering previous records at his base.

When his hitch was up, Sam returned to Curry and got a job driving a truck. In no time Sam's world was shaken badly. The company that employed him went out of business. Then Sam faced the death of his father, whom he idolized. He came apart at his father's bedside, weeping unashamedly as he watched life escape from his father's grasp.

Home was not the same with the senior Piccolo gone, so Sam left Curry and headed for the East Coast. He found a job driving a truck for a baking company in New Jersey, but his heart wasn't in it. He slipped into a pattern of chronic absenteeism, which ended abruptly when he was fired. Jobless and discouraged, he headed back to Pittsburgh to find a new start. He landed a job as a trucker, moving an eighteen-wheeler across eighteen states. He lived the life of a big rig driver until 1964, when he heard of an opening for a crane operator at Pittron Steel Foundry. Sam had never operated a crane. Desperate, he went to one of his friends, who was a skilled crane-man, and asked for a crash course in the art. His friend explained the specifics of crane operation to Sam in detail—but it was all theory, and Sam had no opportunity to practice. Boldly, he applied for the job and took the test for crane operator. Amazing his buddy, but not himself, Sam passed the test and got the job.

The steel foundry was a new world for Piccolo. He was tough, and the difficult working conditions were not foreign to him. But what he found at Pittron appalled him. He could neither believe nor accept the working conditions of the plant. He became a rebel, refusing to submit to the deplorable conditions. Not many men challenged him. Piccolo carried his 212 pounds on a massive frame, and his presence in the plant was duly noticed. His thirty-inch waist is long gone, surrendered to the steelworkers' commitment to Iron City Beer.

Sam wasn't at Pittron long before the union appointed him shop steward for the crane division. Within a year he became a grievance committeeman. In 1970, Piccolo ran for president of USWA Local 1306 and won. Sam went on to win re-election twice, giving him a string of three consecutive terms as president. The first man to win three successive terms since the Local was founded, he became a union power.

This was the man Alderson was called to encounter. Instructions were relayed to Wayne for a secret meeting. The rendezvous was to be held in Room 8 at a nearby Holiday Inn. Alderson vascillated. He knew very well he was not permitted to be involved in such unauthorized meetings. He discussed it with Nancy. She urged him not to go, feeling that too many threats were in the air. It was Sunday, but the scheduled meeting would not be a picnic.

Wayne went anyway. A voice shouted in his mind, *Point man out.* . . . To him, this was war all over again and that motel room was the point. Arriving at the Holiday Inn, Wayne knocked on the door of Room 8. Piccolo motioned him in.

As soon as Wayne entered the room, he knew he had been set up. Piccolo had six of his men with him. There was evidence of heavy drinking. Hostility hung in the air.

Alderson knew he was in trouble. This was an explosive situation. He was not authorized to be there. He had no cover. It was political suicide. He knew it was a "no win" situation.

Piccolo, with his massive barrel chest, glared menacingly at Alderson and shoved a piece of paper into his hand.

"Here's our demands. Meet them and we settle the strike."

Wayne didn't even look at what was written on the paper. Instead, he slowly crumpled it in his fist and threw it at Piccolo's feet, saying defiantly, "I'm not here to talk about demands."

At that point one of Piccolo's black buddies jumped up, obviously drunk, and pulled a switchblade. Playing the "dozens" with Alderson, he spewed forth profanity in which he suggested Wayne was guilty of the worst kind of incest and said, "I'm going to slit your throat, whitey!"

Wayne was scared, but true to form, he threw caution and Christian charity aside. Using the most provocative epithet he knew, he shouted, "Either cut my throat or shut up and sit down before I cut yours, you yellow-bellied bastard!"

Dead silence followed. It was finally broken by Piccolo's measured words,

"OK, we'll settle. This man has balls, like an elephant."

Piccolo had already checked Wayne out thoroughly, and knew that he was a man of his word. He said Alderson was either the dumbest man he'd ever met or the bravest. Perhaps he was a little of both.

The men started to talk in earnest. Wayne asked them to trust him and to judge him on results. He said he wouldn't lie to them or cheat them. Then he telephoned the negotiating officers and asked them to join the meeting. They refused, giving him hell for being there.

Wayne exploded over the phone, "Get over here fast. Forget the protocol. We're going to settle this strike. *Damn it,* he thought, *the back-up troops are still hiding in the woods. . . .*

Minutes later, the officials arrived. Together they worked into the night refining the points of agreement. The next day the men voted to come back and the mill geared up for production. The eighty-four days of strike were over.

# 4

## Operation Turnaround

Wayne Alderson drove his car through the streets of Glassport, passing the storefront churches, ethnic meeting halls, and shops. As he approached the railroad tracks that formed a barrier to the gates of Pittron, he experienced a queasy feeling in his stomach. The strike was over and this was the day he would launch his management dream, Operation Turnaround. His team had been briefed and promises had been made, now it was up to Alderson to make it work. The voices of the skeptics were echoing in Wayne's ears. He knew the vultures were poised, ready to attack at the slightest sign of failure. He had effectively and persuasively "talked the talk," but now it was time to "walk the walk." He crossed the tracks and entered the gate. Operation Turnaround was underway.

The plan called for more than a "rah-rah spirit." Pittron's work force was comprised of grown men and women who would not put up with children's games or empty rhetoric. To cut through to the hearts of those men, who had been hardened by years of growing mistrust and broken promises, would take a strong effort. It meant action that was visible and genuine. There were new promises to keep.

The first step was simple, but dangerous. As a form of announcement, Wayne had huge posters hung strategically throughout the plant. Everywhere the workers looked was a poster that proclaimed Operation Turnaround. The workers knew all about announcements. They were veterans of television, with its glut of advertisements and commercials cloaking deceit in the garb of wonderful promises.

Wayne's announcements were made boldly and widely, so that no one could miss them. In effect they proclaimed, "We shall be different," inviting the closest possible scrutiny from the labor force. Here was the danger—it was put up now or shut up forever. The posters called for mutual cooperation and teamwork between labor and management. A fine idea, but the workers would look to their managers and supervisors to see if anything would really change. Wayne knew posters weren't magic; words on the wall had no power to turn the foundry around. Without demonstrable action, the posters would be so much graffitti.

As a matter of course, when management posted signs in the plant, they became fair game for the angry employees. It was assumed that within twenty-four hours of the posting of signs they would become billboards of profanity reflecting the vented hostilities of the workers. But the Operation Turnaround posters were left untouched. Perhaps the workers clung to a faint hope that this time things would change. To mar these signs would be to desecrate this glimmer of hope they carried within them. The workers waited . . . and watched.

Alderson intuitively understood that the first step toward reconciliation had to come from the management team. They were supposed to be the leaders, the ones invested with the authority and power. It was their responsibility. He also realized that any significant change in the work environment would not take place overnight. The hostility felt by the workers had been long in evolving. The wounds of previous bouts of confrontation were imbedded deeply. Human beings were creatures of habit, and the habit of management by confrontation was difficult to break.

But Alderson, an optimist by nature, did not allow the unfavorable odds to push him to despair. His combat experience provided him with an operational strategy, and he likened Operation Turnaround to the task of capturing a town. You took the town a street at a time, you took the street a house at a time, you took the house a room at a time. If the town were taken quickly, it would be destroyed in the process.

In war, each side knows who the enemy is. But who or what was the enemy at Pittron? The goals of both labor and management were, as always, the same. Both wanted higher productivity. Both wanted increased sales. Both wanted better quality of goods and services. Both would welcome a better work atmosphere. But these goals were not being met because they were so busy fighting each other.

Wayne thought the situation was similar to many marriages he had seen, which had been destroyed by futile confrontation. The marriages did not start out badly; divorce and hatred were not their original goals. In fact, most marriages started with bright hopes, bold promises, and glowing expressions of love and affection. But over the years these warm feelings and sweet expectations were demolished one by one. Eventually, the marriages were destroyed.

The sequence of events in such relationships, whether marriage or of labor and management, follows the route of a spiral rather than a straight line. In marriage, for example, the process is often something like this. The husband insults or violates the wife. In doing so, he robs her of a small part of her womanhood. Now she feels like less of a woman, less capable of complementing her husband, less capable of doing the things he needs to feel like a man. So she retaliates, responding in kind. Her negative response offends the man. Now he feels like less of a man, less capable of doing the things necessary to restore his wife's sense of secure womanhood. Thus he violates her again and the downward spiral picks up speed and moves toward the day when one partner must leave altogether to survive, or turns to a third party for consolation.

Can such a downward spiral in a marriage be healed or redeemed overnight? Candles and roses or a moonlight stroll won't erase years of pain and aggravation. But the *direction* of the spiral can change in five minutes. In marriage, if one partner takes the first step, the spiral can move upward instead of downward. One single act cannot save a marriage, but it can begin the process of turning the spiral around.

That is what Operation Turnaround was all about: turning the Pittron spiral around. He was convinced that if either labor or management continued their conscious commitment to the politics of confrontation, such a commitment would be relational suicide.

Alderson came to the firm conviction that labor was not the enemy of management, and management was not the enemy of labor. Unconsciously, and unwittingly management had become its own worst enemy. By uncritically accepting confrontation as a management tool, it had sown the seeds of its own destruction. Thus Alderson began to attack those assumptions. He sought first not to "correct" labor, but to correct himself, to modify his own management style.

The first step Wayne took was to throw away the scorecard. He committed himself to taking positive steps of reconciliation, expecting nothing in return. If positive responses appeared, they would be viewed as bonuses rather than repaid debts. There would be no marker system if reconciliation was to prevail over confrontation. *It's up to us,* Wayne thought. *We must take the first step and—if necessary—the second and third until things start to change. We're responsible for what we do, not for what they do in response.*

Wayne's next step was to break a cardinal rule of management. He began to walk with the men. Though no company policy manual stated it explicitly, it was tacitly understood that management never walks with labor.

Wayne determined to learn the names of each man, and to become acquainted with him. He was aware of the fact that the men wanted to be recognized, to be known and appreciated for their efforts. The work force numbered slightly over three hundred at the time, making it difficult for individuals to be anything but anonymous. Wayne began walking through the plant daily, stopping to chat with the men as they worked, addressing them by name. Suddenly, the Vice-President in charge of Operations was highly visible. The men began to wonder what was up.

One day, he stopped to watch a chipper. Chippers had one of the hardest jobs in the plant. It was dirty, filthy work, demanding brute strength and endurance. The chipper's tool was a large hammer, like a jack hammer, weighing about thirty pounds, which he used to chip away defects from large steel castings. Some of the castings weighed up to three hundred thousand pounds, and were the size of a small house.

Wayne stopped and shouted up at the man, "Hey, Tony, what are you doing?"

Stifling a curt reply, the man looked at the boss and said simply, "Chipping."

"It looks like hard work."

With a weary glance the Chipper said, "It is."

Alderson said, "Let me have a crack at it."

With that, Wayne removed his suit coat, rolled up his sleeves, and climbed onto the casting. He asked for the hammer. As the chipper watched in disbelief, Wayne began furiously working with the hammer. His stamina lasted all of three minutes. Sweating profusely and gasping for breath, he said to the chipper, "How much money do you get paid for this job?"

The chipper told him, and Wayne breathed a heavy sigh. Shaking his hand, he said, "This is tough work. You earn every cent the company pays you."

Within five minutes every man on the floor had heard about the episode. Alderson, by his gesture, had dignified the least respected task in the plant. It was like a surgeon emptying a bed pan or a banker cleaning the washroom. He left one happy chipper in his wake as he continued his rounds.

Other small, symbolic steps were taken to implement Operation Turnaround, and Wayne broke another industrial tradition. Status was reflected in small but obvious ways within the plant. For example, the color of the safety helmets, the men wore communicated rank and status. Just like in the cowboy movies, where the "good guys" always wore white hats and the "bad guys" wore black hats, in the plant the laborer's hard hat was traditionally dark blue or brown, while the boss's hat was always white. In a consummate act of symbolism, Wayne had his safety helmet painted black. This simple gesture had a galvanizing effect on the men. Ultimately, the hat was treated like a religious relic, enshrined in a case under the open hearth.

The act symbolized the management team's willingness to give up one of their prerogatives. Of course they didn't exchange their white shirts for blue ones; they didn't give up their executive privileges. Wayne didn't move his family out of the suburbs to live near the rank and file. He remained a manager and upheld the dignity of his office. The men didn't want their bosses to start wearing blue shirts. As long as they were respected and recognized, they actually enjoyed the elevated status of their leaders. They began to take special pride in their leaders and wanted them to have more status than leaders of other competitive enterprises. The more status their leaders had, the more significant they felt themselves.

Sam Piccolo, the union president, was the leader on the floor, but his office was not paneled with teak wood. In fact, the only office he had was the cab of his crane. Alderson saw that as a slur on Piccolo's leadership, an insult to his dignity, and took steps to correct the inequity. Piccolo was given a real office in which to meet with his men.

If the rank and file were watching Alderson to detect a false move, Piccolo was like a hawk. He watched and waited, and wondered if Wayne would break. He was impressed, but the jury was still out. After an eighty-four day strike, no union president can afford to be buddy-buddy with a management executive. To be openly friendly would be to provoke suspicions of a sellout, to lose credibility with his men. Piccolo bided his time.

Alderson added another feature to his daily routine: standing at the company gate like a pastor standing by the church door, greeting his parishioners after the Sunday service. As the men came off the shift, Wayne offered his hand and personally thanked each man for his day's work. At first he felt ridiculous standing there, and in the beginning only a few of the men stopped to shake hands. Most avoided him, warily averting their eyes. Gradually, however, the minority grew to a large majority, warmly grasping their boss's hand as they left the plant. The men's response helped Wayne to feel comfortable as he stood there.

With these small but meaningful gestures, Operation Turnaround began to gather momentum. The spiral was beginning to turn upward. Perhaps more importantly, the germ of a new, far-reaching concept was taking shape in Wayne's brain. It emerged as the "Value of the Person" concept. Alderson realized that the key to worker morale and reconciliation focused on how people were being treated. If people were valued, prized more than machines or profits, perhaps the other logistical and mechanical problems of management would begin to take care of themselves. It dawned on him that Pittron's problems were not caused primarily by problems of capital, supplies, or equipment. The problems of Pittron were people problems. Alderson had heard industrial slogans like "People are our most important products," or "We put people first." But he viewed these claims as empty sounds that would dissipate as soon as production pressures became great. But at Pittron, it was starting to be a reality. People were starting to be valued. What industrial magnate could publicly defy the authority of God on the value of a human being? Who would dare stand before his Creator face to face, and argue that profits were more important than people? What manager would stand up in front of his employees and say, "You have no value?"

Thus the concept of the Value of the Person was born in a

steel foundry in Glassport, Pennsylvania. Wayne Alderson found something both labor and management could agree on. Every man and woman in the entire operation had something in common: they all wanted to be valued.

As Wayne began to ponder the significance of his discovery, he was able to isolate three key ingredients that together spelled the Value of the Person. These ingredients, or virtues, were bound up in three common words: love, dignity, and respect. These were the values that had to be restored if Pittron was to make it.

In our culture, love is frequently described in passive terms as something that "happens" to us. It is something over which we have no control. One does not "decide" to fall in love. But Alderson's view of love was different. For him, love had to be involved with doing rather than with feeling. If love is defined by actions rather than feelings, it becomes possible even to love one's enemies.

Creating an atmosphere of love at Pittron did not mean flashing saccharine smiles and using syrupy language. It did not involve turning hard-core realists into plastic imitations of Jesus. It meant simply communicating an attitude through actions that say, "I'm for you."

Previously at Pittron, people communicated that they were *against* each other, living out the *con* of confrontation. Blacks were against whites, labor against management, departments against departments—hardly an environment of love.

To overcome this *contra* mentality, Wayne sought to transcend the issue. Instead of being either pro-labor or pro-management, he began to embody a style that was pro-people. Being *for* people did not mean the end of discipline. It did not mean giving approval to every action or submitting to every demand. It did not convey a weak kind of love that indulged every individual's desire. It was tough love, one that called for excellence and extra effort. This was a steel foundry; if love was to be implemented, it had to be as tough as the tasks of the plant.

How does one communicate that he is *for* people? At Pittron, it meant not merely *feeling* concern for people but *showing* it in visible, concrete, daily actions. Management showed such concern when the workers were all being personally affected by the gasoline shortage that hit the nation in 1974. While its workers were enduring the daily frustrations of waiting in long lines at the gas stations, and at times being greeted by the news that local operators were out of gas, Pittron was amassing nearly six thousand gallons of gasoline. Other companies had similar surpluses in storage, which they guarded carefully, at times having armed men "riding shotgun" on their gas trucks.

Wayne approached his management team with the idea of sharing Pittron's gas reserve with the employees. The discussion provoked some negative responses—not only to the gas sharing plan, but to the whole idea of a new management style. A few of the managers did not back Wayne on the Value of the Person concept. Some thought Operation Turnaround was becoming too risky, afraid of the "give an inch, take a mile" syndrome. They thought management was starting to display a soft underbelly that would weaken and perhaps even destroy its future bargaining position. The unions were tough, they argued, and management had to be tougher. The corporate hawks and doves were starting to take sides.

The debate centered on the gasoline issue. Alderson's plan was simple: make the gasoline available to the employees. He devised an honor system whereby any employee would be permitted to drive up to the pump and request a given number of gallons. The gas was to be provided with no questions asked. The people had different needs. Some drove over a hundred miles a day to and from work; others had family matters to take care of. The honor plan made no distinctions between business or personal use, whatever amount was requested would be given.

A few of the executives were horrified. To some it smelled of a giveaway program and made people wonder if Alderson was becoming weak; others were sure there would be riots at the pump and mobs fighting for gas. The most common objection was that Pittron would run out of gas. When the pumps failed, the plant would have to halt production. Such a disaster might even close the place forever. But Alderson remained firm and finally the president of the company, who had at first voiced strong objections to the idea, relented and backed Wayne's right to run the operation.

Wayne's decision to act was eventually supported by the majority of the management team, and the announcement was made to the employees. The place became a rumor mill, with all kinds of stories circulating about how much the company was going to charge for the gas. Workers suspected a management move designed to exploit the ancient law of supply and demand. One worker confronted Wayne on the floor.

"How much will the gas cost? I'm not about to pay anyone a dollar a gallon for gas no matter how much I need it."

Wayne replied, "Nothing—the gas is free."

Somehow, the announcement had failed to mention that the gas was being offered *free.* The workers could hardly believe it. Word quickly spread through the plant and into the town of Glassport. The news media showed up in time to see Wayne pumping gas into the employees' cars. One of them shouted, "Why are you doing this?" "Why not?" Wayne replied.

The answer became a buzz word in the plant. Robert Kennedy's slogan became a reality at Pittron: "Some men look at challenges and ask 'why?' Others look and ask, 'why not?' "

Despite the prophets of doom, the honor system worked. There were no riots, no shoving matches at the pump. One man drove up to the pump and requested one gallon. Many asked for no more than two. Some were so low on gas they ran out before they reached their goal and had to be pushed to the pumps.

The worst fear, however, was realized: Pittron ran out of gas. An executive burst into Wayne's office with the news, exclaiming, "It happened. We ran out of gas. Now what do we do?"

Wayne was stunned. He didn't know what to do. He had no answer. But he was saved by a smiling Providence when, like a *deus ex machina* in a Greek drama, the phone rang. The voice on the other end asked Wayne, "Are you the guy giving away free gas to your employees?"

"Yes," Wayne said.

"That's unbelievable. Look, I have two thousand gallons of gas on hand. Do you want them?"

Those were sweet words. With the replenished supply and the easing of the national shortage, Pittron was able to continue and Operation Turnaround made another leap forward. Free gas had communicated to the men and their families that Pittron was "for" them. The six thousand gallons of gas were gone, but in its place was emerging a corps of people who were being mobilized to become a model of labor-management harmony.

Maintaining this atmosphere of active love meant protecting the dignity of the worker. Wayne realized that the question of human dignity was becoming paramount in America. From the civil rights movement to Lordstown, the same basic issue was cropping up. Alderson was only vaguely aware of the attention given the problem by the social scientists, philosophers, and psychologists—to Wayne, the name B. F. Skinner sounded like a horse trader. The only thing this child of the coal fields could envision "beyond freedom and dignity" was slavery and indignity.

There were no deep philosophical discussions about dignity at Pittron; most of the work force would have been hard pressed to give a verbal definition of the word. But they understood *in*dignity. They knew what it was like to feel the loss of personal worth. For them, the question of dignity was an issue of the gut, not of the mind. When workers said they were treated like animals they were talking about dignity.

Alderson looked for answers to his own questions about human dignity. He had heard the theories, seen the films, and read the novels. He got the message that was making the rounds —the message that man was just another animal, a naked ape who emerged from the slime through the forces of blind chance. He heard that man was a cosmic accident suited ultimately only for death and annihilation. But he didn't believe it. He wasn't ready to embrace a philosophy of suicide.

Nor was Wayne willing to rest his confidence in the reality of human dignity on the basis of sentiment. He was smart enough to realize that if man's origin were in insignificance and his destiny were equally insignificant, he couldn't possibly have real dignity in the brief span we call life. If that were so, then the tombstone tells it all—date born, date died. Wayne figured it was what happened between those dates that mattered— particularly when it dealt with people and their work. He didn't want to lead a work force that was "tired of livin' and scared of dyin'."

Thus Wayne found more and more ways to demonstrate to the workers that they were important; that not only did their work count, *they* counted. Wayne began to visit them in their homes in times of trouble. Workers convalescing after a serious illness were surprised to see their vice-president in charge of operations at their front door. They knew such activities were not spelled out in his job description. Wayne's presence made a profound impact on them. They were being treated as persons instead of mules. Foundry manager Jim Goebel echoed the question, "Why not?"

"Why shouldn't we be concerned about them? We are all human beings. We all have the same problems, the same fears, the same weaknesses. What does it cost to take the extra second to ask a man about his wife or his kids? Fact is, I wondered how his wife was doing."

It wasn't hard for Wayne to find out whose family was hurting. When a man's wife or child was hospitalized or there was a death in the family, the company knew it. As a matter of course, medical insurance forms and death benefit files were processed by the personnel department. Wayne set up a routine whereby he was notified of such family crises. He made it a practice to stop at the hospital or the funeral parlor on the way home from work. This kind of activity pulled the pin for an explosion of increased worker morale. The bosses were giving

their most jealously guarded possession—their personal time—
to say that these people were important. And why not? Many
of them were already long since committed to giving long hours
to their favorite charitable causes.

Wayne's team was busy communicating respect for every
person in the plant, believing that respect for other people is
closely related to self-respect. Nothing destroys both faster than
negative criticism. Wayne had been told all his life to be open
to constructive criticism. He was told not to be defensive when
critics ripped into him with fury. Criticism was given "for his
own good," but somehow he found that difficult to believe. As
he thought about it, he realized that a lot of criticism he had
received was not constructive, but destructive. It hurt him
more than it helped him. He remembered, with pain, that
when he was a boy one of his teachers said to him, "You'll never
amount to anything."

Perhaps that is partly what drove him to volunteer for the
point in the war. He had to prove her wrong. When his classmates had a vote for "most likely to succeed," Wayne was sure
he didn't receive a single vote. He was just happy there wasn't
a vote for "most likely to fail."

At Pittron, negative criticism prevailed. Insults were commonplace, and management had acquired a "red pencil mentality." The men were tired of being called derogatory names.
The black man bristled at the word "nigger"; the Slavic person
was weary of being called a "polack" or a "hunky"; the Italian
fumed at the name "dago." This atmosphere of insult and negative criticism had to change if Operation Turnaround was going
to continue its upward spiral.

Wayne felt it necessary to earn respect rather than demand
it with a club. He had heard of Teddy Roosevelt's famous
maxim, "Walk softly and carry a big stick," and had been part
of a management philosophy that bought the big stick creed.
The big stick says, "If you do not like me, if you do not love me,
at least you will respect me because of my power." The big stick
mentality, however does not produce respect, but fear.

Wayne threw away his stick. Instead of criticisms, he looked for ways to encourage the men by genuine compliments. The men knew the difference between a real compliment and flattery, between love and patronage. Flattery was mere deceit designed to manipulate and use people. Wayne's compliments had the ring of truth rather than the hollow sound of flattery.

This didn't mean that constructive criticism or performance evaluations were abandoned. Simply, the *tone* was changed. People were respected and everyone noticed it. Wayne understood that the human ego is the most fragile of mechanisms and should not be trampled on. Statements like, "You are mandated," "You are required," "You must," were deleted from memos. This was the language of the big stick, of confrontation, which invariably evoked hostile reactions. Men wanted to be treated like men, not children. White men don't like being called "boy" any more than black men do.

In the arena of labor and management, every person wants to experience the respect of fellow workers, subordinates, peers, and bosses. Alderson sensed that need and desire deeply rooted in the rank and file; he soon came to realize that management had the same need.

The work force tended to look on management as "pansies." They were the people who really never worked, yet they were in the seats of authority and status. They were people to be envied, not respected. They had it made.

Alderson knew management wasn't like that. He sat on a seat of authority, but it was also a hot seat of responsibility—the kind that produces ulcers, coronaries, and valium addiction. Not too many rank and file were hooked on tranquilizers. That was a management syndrome, more common than the three martini lunch. With management went the anxiety and insecurity that accompanies a profound sense of loneliness. Where the buck stops, mercy stops, and Wayne knew it. It was management that bore the burden of the bottom line. It was management that faced the daily terror that goes with decision making. In the hot summers in Pittsburgh, many of the foundry laborers had difficulty sleeping in the oppressive heat of their houses without air conditioning. But the managers were unable to sleep in spite of their comforts. They tossed and turned and sweated, not because of the heat of the night, but because of the weight of the decisions they faced the next day. Every manager knew that status and economic rewards are not enough to make a person happy. They were human beings too. They also craved love, dignity, and respect. The Value of the Person could only work at Pittron if it included everyone.

Wayne found ways to give recognition to both labor and management. He tried to communicate to each person that his task benefited the total operation of the plant. Wayne followed the maxim, "Respect a man's family and you respect the man. Show interest in the things he cares about and you show interest in him." An incident at Pittron illustrated this. One of the men related, "It was during the early days of Operation Turnaround. I was working overtime and was allowed to leave the plant to eat. I left by the Sixth Street Gate, which was against regulations. I went home to eat with my wife. I lingered a bit and was running late, so she drove me back to the foundry.

"She dropped me off at the same gate which connects with the main office. I jumped out of the car and ran for the door. As I went through the door, I saw Mr. Alderson coming down the stairs. I was petrified. He stopped and grabbed me by the arm. He asked, 'Was that you who just jumped out of that car and came running over here?' I admitted that it was and started to apologize. Just then Mr. Alderson's secretary came along and he said to her, 'I was watching this man from the window of the conference room. Do you know what he just did? He just ran in here without even bothering to kiss his wife goodbye.' Then he turned to me and said, 'How could you do that? If she were still here I'd make you go back out there and kiss her goodbye.'

"I explained to Mr. Alderson that I was late and didn't want to get into trouble with my job. Then Mr. Alderson said, 'Don't ever think that your job is more important than your wife.' Those words really stuck with me."

Such incidents were not recorded merely by the rank and file. They occurred with management as well.

Wayne noticed that one of his managers was spending an unusual amount of time at the plant. At first he assumed that the man was merely caught up in Operation Turnaround, but office rumors soon got back to Wayne that the man's marriage was in trouble. This was confirmed when he received a phone call from the manager's wife. She told him that her husband was never home. He was spending a lot of time at the foundry, but even more time frequenting many of the twenty-eight bars that are found in Glassport. The woman asked Wayne to help her get her husband back.

Alderson met with the manager in his office. He reduced his hours and gave him special time off to spend with his wife. He told him he could not do a good job of managing men on the floor if he was neglecting his family. The man took Wayne seriously, following a plan Alderson outlined, and got his house in order. The marriage is still intact and both husband and wife have a continued sense of gratitude for the extra care they received. Not surprisingly, as the man improved his relationship with his wife and family, his performance as a manager showed a measurable improvement.

A spirit of teamwork blossomed, which benefited even the wives and children of the workers. Love, dignity, and respect were being incarnated in visible action in the antiquated, grimy steel foundry.

What did Operation Turnaround achieve? How did it affect the actual operation of the plant? The owners of Pittron were not interested in hearing about sweetness and light, and about what a nice place Pittron was becoming. They wanted to know the bottom line: measurable results.

The scorecard for Operation Turnaround's twenty-one month history went like this: (1) sales went up 400 percent; (2) profits rose to 30 percent; (3) employment went up 300 percent (the work force grew to over one thousand employees); (4) productivity rose 64 percent; (5) labor grievances declined from as many as twelve per week to one per year; (6) chronic absenteeism virtually disappeared; and (7) quality of the product became the best in the history of the plant.

Pittron had suddenly become the Cadillac of the steel foundry industry, exceeding the goals of the five-year plan the owners said would never work. Of Textron's thirty-five divisions, Pittron moved from last place to the top ten. The results were astonishing, but they were real and they were measurable. No one could deny them. Pittron's solid bottom line was every manager's dream. G. William Miller was ecstatic. He said, "There will never be a penalty for over-achievement."

Other corporations began inquiring about the causes of the dramatic turnaround. Pittron's story attracted national attention. News of it even reached the White House, via Lefty Scumaci. It emerged as a vital challenge to the sacrosanct managerial philosophy of confrontation. The sacred cow of alienation had been slaughtered on Pittron's alter of reconciliation. The Value of the Person had shown that there was "a more excellent way."

In the short space of twenty-one months, Pittron moved from a deficit of six million dollars to a profit of six million dollars— a profit-loss swing of twelve million dollars. Business speculators couldn't ignore such obvious success. Storm clouds were forming on the distant horizon, which the men of Pittron knew nothing about. They would find out soon enough.

# 5

## The Miracle of Pittron

When Wayne Alderson entered the gates of Pittron after the strike, he did not go in alone; he resolved to bring his God along. Not that God had and needed Wayne to give Him access to the foundry, or that security guards and barbed wire would ever keep Him out. Rather, God came in a special way, a way that was visible and tangible. Wayne Alderson took his faith out of mothballs and let it be seen in the mill.

Wayne quickly gained the reputation for being "religious," but his religious profile does not fit the standard mold. It is rough-hewn, spontaneous, and earthy. At times the coarseness of his language, bred in the rough environment of industry, is offensive to the legions of the "born again." Like Luther before him, his speech is seasoned with salt and then some. A few, who cannot look into the inner chamber of his soul, mistake him for a profane man.

Alderson is not a clergyman. His parish is the marketplace, the board room, the shop floor. He has no interest in theology, but he knows God. His personal faith is tenacious, able to withstand the hammering of the skeptical and hostile. That his spiritual drive is as real as it is complex can be denied by no one who knows him.

In a word, Alderson is different. His strong individualism is interpreted variously by observers. To some his style appears vain and self-centered, a sign of spiritual immaturity; to others he appears bold and innovative. Which, if either, is correct, is a judgment best left to God. Where Wayne goes, his passionate faith goes as well—that he will not compromise.

Operation Turnaround was not a religious program by design. Alderson never saw himself as an evangelist. He had a personal aversion to anyone "shoving religion down his throat," and didn't want to be guilty of doing it to others. His vocation was to be Vice-President of Operations of a steel foundry.

What began as an inward spiritual adventure for Wayne soon took on outward shape. It happened simply enough. Early in the days of Operation Turnaround, Sam Piccolo engaged Wayne in small talk. The conversation turned to religion. Piccolo had no religious leanings, but was intrigued by Wayne's behavior and the new spirit that was moving over the plant. He probed Wayne to find out what he was made of.

"Pic" was not merely indifferent toward religion, he was, in fact, hostile. He had been hurt by the Church. He had gone to church as a boy, but drifted away as he grew older. When he was divorced, he was excommunicated. He didn't understand the whys and wherefores of Church discipline. All he knew was that he had been drummed out of the corps. He was bruised by that and the hurt twisted into anger and bitterness. His feelings toward Alderson were ambivalent; his respect for Wayne collided with his wariness of religion. He was quick with the jibes and barbs of a man made uncomfortable by the presence of a religious person.

Their conversation about religion took place in front of the open hearth. Showers of sparks sprayed them as they exchanged guarded banter. Piccolo yelled above the din of the roaring furnace and clanging machinery, "Hey Wayne T.—

how'd you get to know so much about the Bible? From a hangin'
judge?"

Alderson grinned and answered back, jibe for jibe. He was
getting used to Piccolo's favorite names for him—"Black Hat,"
"Long-legged preacher man," "Ichabod Crane," "Lanky."
Wayne was aware that behind the jive talk was more than a hint
of the respect of one strong man for another.

Wayne kept the banter going. "Hey Pic—you can read the
fine print of labor contracts; you're a walking encyclopedia
when it comes to that stuff. Why can't you read the Bible?"

As abruptly as it started, the joking about the Bible ended.
Embarrassed, they changed the subject to more mundane matters.

However, their muted conversation had been overheard by
one of the men. Vince Slavik went to his locker and hauled out
the shopworn Bible he read every day. He came to Wayne and
Sam and showed it to them. Explaining that he had overheard
their conversation, he politely challenged them to meet together for informal study of the Bible. Wayne dodged the challenge with the words, "Yeh, that would be nice."

And changed the subject again.

As soon as the conversation was over, Wayne dismissed the
idea from his head. Piccolo didn't. He went and talked it over
with a few of his men. They waited to spring it on Alderson
again.

A few days later, Wayne was walking the foundry floor at
lunchtime. Piccolo was huddled with his men over coffee and
sandwiches when Alderson approached them. Using his half-
empty thermos as a pointer, Pic started needling Wayne again.

"Hey preacher man—you ready to start teachin' us about the
Bible?"

Wayne parried the thrust of Piccolo's jabbing thermos,
watching to see if inertia might spill the remaining coffee in his
direction. There was no doubt in Alderson's mind that Pic and
his men were just having a little fun at his expense. Wayne
didn't mind, as the cost of such fun was far outweighed by the

value of the rapport that was developing. He laughed, "I'll bet you guys want a Bible study!"

This was the second time the idea was mentioned, but Alderson interpreted it as a harmless kind of fun-poking at him. Wayne was still not used to living with a high profile religious image. He tried to master the art of absorbing this sort of ribbing, without appearing either brittle or saccharine about it.

The next day brought the charm of the third try. Wayne returned to Piccolo and his men with a pocket-sized New Testament tucked away inside his jacket, evidencing the slightest bulge, which to these men might suggest the ludicrous idea that he was "carrying." *Just maybe,* he thought, *They might be serious.*

Again Piccolo mentioned a Bible study, but this time he wasn't laughing. When he asked Wayne about it, he looked him right in the eye. Wayne had seen that look in the Holiday Inn during the strike, and he knew immediately that Piccolo was serious.

"If that's really what you guys want, it's okay with me."

Sam said, "Where and when? You name the place and we'll be there."

"How about right here, right now?"

Piccolo was stunned. He didn't think Wayne would really "cross the line" and do this with the men.

Wayne opened his testament to Romans, Chapter Twelve. The men read it together. It dealt with hatred and vengeance, of returning good for evil. It spoke of being transformed rather than being conformed to this world. It carried the Apostle Paul's message of a strange kind of nonconformity, a nonconformity that responded to hate with love, to evil with good, that left vengeance up to God rather than men.

Like the small crowds that gather to watch adversaries square off in debate, the men stood staring at their plant vice-president and their union president sitting at a table with a Bible open between them. Alderson and Piccolo, huddling over a book, were oblivious to the spectators, talking in animated fashion about what they were reading. This was not a bargaining table or an occasion for reading a grievance petition. Labor and management were together not for negotiating economic benefits, but to be instructed in a "more excellent way."

The onlookers were baffled by the strange sight before their eyes. They shifted their feet awkwardly, raised their eyebrows, and some even pointed at Wayne and Pic while covering their mouths with their hands to suppress a mocking laugh. But nobody laughed out loud. It was too unusual a sight to be rudely disrupted by laughter. Hidden in their embarrassed amusement were the deep-rooted remnants of hope they didn't want to spoil.

One of Pic's men spoke up, declaring boldly, "I don't hate anybody. I just can't stand the son of a bitch that works next to me."

The men laughed, and confessed they had enjoyed the casual informal discussion. They decided to do it again. The six of them agreed to meet every Wednesday on their lunch break. It would be open-ended, with no formal agenda. Their meeting place would be a storage room alongside the open hearth.

The six men continued to meet there for three consecutive weeks. By the third week, the group had become so large that the storage room wouldn't hold them.

Sam came to Wayne with an idea. "If we are going to keep this Bible Class, we better get a bigger place. I know a spot that might work out."

With that, Piccolo led Wayne to a section of the foundry he had never seen in the eight years he had been with Pittron. The new spot was an old abandoned storage room, situated directly under the open hearth. When Wayne saw the place he said immediately, "You're right, this is it. This will be our meeting place."

The site could only be described as the most dismal area of the foundry. It looked like the catacombs where Christians once worshipped in secret as they sought to avoid the persecutors of the Roman Empire. This was no gothic cathedral, there were no stained glass windows. In fact, there were no windows of any kind under the open hearth. The ceiling was low and lighting almost nonexistent. Obsolete scrap, discarded years before, was stacked throughout. The roof was supported by concrete columns stained by water seepage, which made the atmosphere cold and damp. Between the columns were strung the webs of spiders whose daily spinning had gone uninterrupted for years. The spiders were easily evicted and their webs swept clean, but rats presented a more serious problem. The men found stray cats and brought them in to be their sergeant-at-arms for their new meeting hall. Makeshift benches were constructed and the place was ready.

In spite of the crude and dismal surroundings, this was a place the men could be comfortable. No ties were required, no dress code enforced. People could come and go as they pleased. Attendance was never taken, no offering plates passed. This was a voluntary meeting place, created by the men for their own use on their own time. It was theirs, and they began to take special pride in it.

The men began to refer to the meeting place as their "chapel-under-the-open-hearth." An electrician, Lou Bruno, decided to make a sign. He cut out an arrow from a cardboard box and painted it red. Balanced on top was a handmade sign that said simply, *Chapel.* The arrow pointed the way.

Lou Bruno embodied the new spirit that was becoming contagious. His wife, Betty, was beginning to wonder what her husband was up to. She noticed that he was singing in the morning as he stood before the mirror shaving. She was used to hearing him curse as he went out the door for work. Now he was humming. Lou made sure each Wednesday that the lighting was right in the chapel and the benches were dusted. His pride in the place grew steadily.

Others made contributions to the chapel. Men like Vic Briskie, George Townsend, and Harry Reed fashioned figures of a fish from a sand mold. As the early Christian Church used this symbol during worship in the catacombs, so these handmade

Wayne conducting Bible discussion with men of Pittron. June 1973.

symbols were carefully affixed to columns around the plant indicating the route to the chapel.

The signs were not wasted on the men. Within weeks scores of men were making their way underground for the meeting. Labor and management alike met together in a new environment of discussion and dialogue. Amidst the clatter of lunch pails and thermos bottles, and the blue haze of cigarette and cigar smoke, Wayne gave a simple, direct, and brief exposition of a passage from the New Testament. The accent was on the application of New Testament principles to the daily lives and practical problems of men. Sectarian and denominational differences were set aside.

Some who gathered there were regular churchgoers. There were Baptists, Methodists, Lutherans, Pentecostals, Presbyterians, Roman Catholics, people from every conceivable church background. Some were from the Jewish faith. Wayne didn't know what the men's backgrounds were and he didn't ask. It simply was never an issue. Many were people who had not been in a church for years, some were atheists, others agnostics.

The men didn't have any Bibles, so Wayne visited the Salvation Army to see if they could help. The Salvation Army official asked, "What church are you from?"

"No church," Alderson replied, "I'm from the Pittron Steel foundry."

The officer's eyebrows went up at this unusual request. He laughed as he filled out the order for six hundred paperback editions of *Good News for Modern Man,* which he sold Wayne for twenty-four cents apiece. The men now had Bibles and the chapel was complete.

Not everyone came. Wayne insisted that no subtle pressure nor discrimination be imposed upon those who chose not to attend. The voluntary character of the meetings was strictly upheld—Wayne knew that enforced religion was an intolerable tyranny.

At first a wary skepticism kept many of the men away. Jokes about "holyrollers" and "sissy stuff" were rampant at the beginning. Within a short time, however, curiosity began to get the best of them. Men began to stroll in and sit in the back just to see what was going on. Most of those who came once came again and became regulars; men like Vernyi, Rudy, Willie, "Popeye," and "Big Apple."

Scores became hundreds as the walls of skepticism began to crumble. Many who never attended became supporters of the concept, defending the right of their fellow workers to meet on their own time. They applauded the new spirit of cooperation and reconciliation that so obviously emanated from the room under the open hearth.

The lives of many of the men who attended were changed by the experience. No one's story was more dramatic than that of Jim Mordecki. His life was turned upside down by the meetings.

Mordecki was a second generation foundry worker, whose father had worked in the plant for thirty years as a chipper. Quitting school after the tenth grade, young Jim entered the work world. He was determined not to work at the foundry, which the locals referred to as a god-damned place. Jim sought refuge in the landscaping business. But that venture only lasted two years, and Mordecki finally wound up punching in one morning at Pittron. For fifteen years he worked near his father as a molder. Together, the Mordecki's amassed forty-five years of service to the foundry.

Mordecki was not interested in religion. He was turned off. His brother had recently had a religious experience, and it was beginning to annoy him. He began to resent his brother and told him not to bug him about it. Then he started hearing the rumors about the Bible Study starting at work. He wanted no part of it; he was sure it was a management game.

"I knew the corruption of this place. I thought, *Ain't this somethin', now they're going to try religion to get at us. It has to be a gimmick.*"

Mordecki refused to attend. But finally the scuttlebutt on the floor got to him and he decided to see for himself. He went in hostile, looking for flaws, trying to figure the angle Alderson was playing.

"I came out of there overwhelmed. No one talked about work schedules or increased quotas. It was plain to me as Mr. Alderson spoke that he had love in him. I knew I had to go back. I couldn't stay away."

This was a time of crisis in Mordecki's life. He had adopted patterns he knew were self-destructive, spending four to five hours a day with a bottle. A shot and a beer were not enough for him, he had to get drunk. Mordecki had become a "mean drunk." Often he would come home cursing, venting his drunken anger on his wife, Tami, who became the victim of Mordecki's daily frustration.

But as Pittron started to change, so did Mordecki. With the encouragement found in the chapel, the support of his brother and his new pastor, John Creeks, Mordecki began to make it back.

"Tension and frustration were surely leaving the mill," he recalls. "It started to leave my life as well. Suddenly I found I didn't need the bottle anymore. The entire atmosphere of our home changed. My wife says I'm a different person. She is glad."

Mordecki's skepticism vanished with his hostility. He began to believe that Operation Turnaround was for real. It could work. It was working. Jim noticed that he was taking a different attitude toward his own job.

"My work changed. I put more of myself into it. I knew before how to do a job that passes. All I cared about was getting my quotas filled and past the inspectors in quality control. Now I started to do my job with special care. Now it had to pass my own inspection standards. I took pride in what I was doing."

During this time Jim's father died, permanently separating the team of Mordecki and Mordecki. Just as things were taking an upward swing for him, grief intruded into Jim's life. As his father's body was prepared for viewing, Jim and Tami went to the funeral home. When they entered the parlor, the first person to greet them was Wayne. He had no profound words, and was awkward in giving condolences. Rather, he just put his arm on Jim's shoulder. "I don't know what to say, Jim, words aren't very helpful here."

This incident—this simple visit of compassion—made Mordecki a total believer in the Value of the Person. "Mr. Alderson didn't just *say* he cared, he *showed* he cared. He could have had the company send flowers or a sympathy card. He could have done nothing. But he was there personally—on his own time. That said it all for me."

Mordecki's story is echoed by many other workers. Deacon Lunsford, the grandson of slaves, typifies the attitude of men who rejoiced at Pittron's new atmosphere. He was an integral part of the foundry's spiritual renaissance. After Deacon's grandparents died at age 110 and 105, his father gave up share-cropping in Georgia and came north, finding a job in a steel mill. In 1951 the Deacon came to Pittron. His job was difficult and monotonous. He was a chipper involved in the manufac-ture of gun turrets for tanks. He remembers what work was like in the past: "Chip and grind, chip and grind . . . that was my life. The supervisor didn't treat us like men. They called me 'nig-ger.' If we broke our chipping chisels we weren't allowed to resharpen them. We were like the children of Israel. We were allowed no straw for our bricks. The bosses stood over us like prison guards."

Deacon loved the chapel; he felt that God was in the place. And his affection for Wayne was profound.

"God sent us a man. He sent us Mr. Alderson to show how men could work together. He came in wearing a black helmet and called me 'brother.' No white man had ever called me brother. He was like Martin Luther King to us. They should give him a Nobel Prize. If they don't, that's all right. God will give him a prize. He will give him a crown. He is God's man."

The praise went on and on. A crane operator said, "I don't know what heaven is like, but it sounds like what's happening here. I travel 120 miles a day back and forth to work. I enjoy it here. This morning I broke down on the way in. If that had happened before I'd have said, 'forget it,' and gone back home. But I knew the men needed me. And I needed them so I made sure I got here."

"Rev" Bernie, a shot blaster, said, "The foundry is a new place altogether. It's a different place. It is a pleasure to work here. Now a man wants to give something back to the foundry. We call it a fair day's work."

Benny Constantino, the union vice-president, said, "If you told me two years ago that I was going to be working under the conditions I'm working under now, I would never believe it. It's a beautiful place to walk into."

Norval Boyd, chairman of the grievance committee remarked, "It's like walking out of a dark room into daylight."

"Open hearth Sam" spoke between breaths as he shoved a ramming rod against the cold ladle. "Just because they're nice to us doesn't mean you don't have to work hard. Matter of fact, we do more work and we're proud of it."

Shelby Rowe, a chipper, described the working conditions of the past as "dark, dreadful, and miserable. It was slave labor. A man didn't have time to breathe. It was like a horse race with time watches. I'm not a horse, I'm a man."

Shelby never missed a Bible Study. He looked forward to it every week, and always left with his face shining. "You know what happened one day? One of the managers came down on the floor. He stopped to talk to me. I was breathing heavy. He said to me, 'Are you tired?' I said, 'I surely am.' He said to me plain as day, 'Well, take a rest.' It was like a dream."

The manager was Dave Salvi, a man with forty-eight years in management. His father, Frank, had been a chipper for forty-nine years. Salvi understood.

These statements sound extravagant. They do not reflect expressions of cool analysis; they express raw emotion. Men who work in steel foundries are capable of strong passion. That passion may be channeled in the direction of bitterness and rage, but these same men are equally capable of expressing strong emotions in another direction. Their sense of gratitude can be equally intense. Men who labor in a place like Pittron are hard to fool. They do not take kindly to people who try to play games with them, and are able to spot hypocrisy in a minute.

The chapel continued to grow in size and impact, becoming a place where labor and management could meet together as equals. Here there was no bargaining table; under the open hearth no pressure was applied for production quotas or quality control. No grievances were filed here; no progress charts were on display. Worker benefits were not on the agenda. Here men were trying to understand a little bit about who God is and who they were as human beings. They discovered that people in management have the same kind of personal problems, struggles, and aspirations the hourly workers have. They discovered their bosses were human beings, not prison wardens hired by the owners to torment them.

Supervisors became aware of their men as human beings. Instead of viewing them as slots on an assembly line, or bodies at the ends of shovels, they grew to know them as real people. They gained an increased awareness of the workers as husbands and fathers. They became interested in their family lives. In the chapel, the distinction between labor and management was not obliterated, but many of the dividing walls between them were knocked down. The chapel became the most visible symbol of Operation Turnaround. God was in the plant.

*NOVEMBER 9, 1973.* In the midst of Pittron's renaissance, the shouts of joy and acclamation were abruptly silenced when a fire hit the plant. This was no ordinary fire—it was a vicious, explosive inferno that poured liquid fire over the foundry floor like a volcano.

Molten steel, used for filling gigantic molds, was contained in huge ladles. Each ladle had a mouth eight feet wide and held up to one hundred thousand pounds of liquid metal. These ladles were moved by cranes high above the foundry floor, following a path from the furnace to a mold, where their contents were carefully poured like steaming coffee into a cup. The heat of the molten steel registered twenty-seven hundred degrees Fahrenheit.

On November 9, a "triple-header" was being poured. This involved three heats of almost identical size, weight, and temperature. The procedure, though dangerous, was controlled by a wide variety of mechanical devices in addition to human supervision and was considered routine. During the pouring process, the ladle was emptied into a mold by means of a runner cup. The ladle was locked into pouring position by use of sleeves, which are called "stoppers." The stoppers were then opened slowly, producing an even, steady flow of liquid steel. Once the flow was consistent, the rest was automatic.

But the triple-header of November 9 was anything but routine. No one knows exactly what happened. Somewhere between the furnace and the mold there was an ominous malfunction that produced what the workers call a "leaker." As the men started the first pour, they couldn't close the stoppers. The steel began to spill over the foundry floor. Like lava spewing from the jaws of a volcano, eighty-five thousand pounds of liquid fire poured out of control in the sixty-foot bay area. Men were screaming and running in the shower of flames. The molten steel was five inches deep on the floor, turning it into a blazing incinerator. Flames roared toward the ceiling where gas and oxygen lines were protected by a thin layer of corrugated siding. Only seconds were left before a massive explosion would blow up the building.

During the pour, twelve men were in the immediate vicinity. Their chances for survival in such a catastrophe were next to nothing. As the spillage began, they left their posts and frantically tried to escape the inevitable holocaust. Overhead a craneman, Ralph Wright, was trying desperately to get out of his cab before he was burned alive. Although he swears to this day that he didn't touch a thing, in his frenzy to escape he must have bumped the trolly lever of the crane, sending the spilling ladle hurtling safely away from the people underneath it. This "accident" bought seconds of precious time. The ladle moved at full speed down the trolley line until it crashed into the bumpers of the crane and abruptly stopped. Inertia did the rest. What fire remained in the ladle poured out as it was brought to a jerking halt. Now the fire was burning out of control at both ends of the sixty foot bay.

Ralph Wright, coughing and blinded by the smoke, groped for a ladder as he tried to get out of the crane. Wright negotiated the ladder and tried to move along a catwalk. Barely eighteen inches wide and with no railings, the walkway was rendered even more perilous by cross-beams that obstructed it every twenty feet. Wright couldn't see, but he had to keep moving or it would mean certain death. His options were grim. The electrician, who had been stationed above for safety reasons, made it to the catwalk in time to prevent him from falling. He grabbed Wright's hand and led him safely to a platform out of danger. It was like walking a tightrope over hell.

Meanwhile, the ladle kept pouring liquid fire on the floor, consuming everything in its path. Wooden and steel lockers lined the sides of the bay. The wooden lockers were turned to ashes and the steel lockers were melted. The contents of the lockers were annihilated by the heat. Hardhats and safety shoes with steel toes were turned into cinders.

Someone rushed to shut off the flow of oxygen and gas only seconds before the fire ate through the corrugated siding. Likewise, someone else shut off the electrical power. Nothing more could be done; only time could bring the fire under control. The fire was left to burn itself out.

When it was over, the foundry floor had a ghostly look of doomsday about it. Lockers twisted out of shape, a dangling ladle, charred ashes everywhere; it was a scene of total devastation. Incredibly, there were no bodies. Every man present when the spillage started had escaped. The few seconds Wright's "accident" bought them were enough for them to get out. Not one man on the floor was injured. Ralph Wright washed his eyes out with water, took a few breaths of fresh air and was ready to go back to work. The Pittsburgh papers called it a miracle.

The men set about the arduous task of cleaning up the debris that was left from the fire. George Protz, an immigrant from Czechoslovakia, moved slowly toward what was left of his locker. He waded through the rubble, kicking aside debris with his bull-like legs and feet, noting that every flammable object was burnt to a crisp. He had little hope of salvaging anything from his locker, which had been in the center of the fire. In fact, it was difficult for him to distinguish his locker from the others

—all of them seemed to be welded into one grotesque mass of twisted metal. Prying the door open, he was astounded at what he saw in front of him. There was his paperback edition of the New Testament, completely intact. The edge of the cover was slightly singed, but the book itself was unmarred. Right beside the Bible were the melted remains of a pair of steel-toed shoes and what once had been a hard hat. Everything else in the locker was completely burned.

George Protz grabbed the book with his rough hands and clutched it to his chest like a holy relic. His hands were trembling and his eyes moist as the burly steel worker was frozen to the spot in silent emotion. He felt as if the book were alive in his hands, as if it were speaking out loud.

George Protz carried the Bible to Alderson the next day and related his story. Alderson was deeply moved.

"To me it was God saying to the whole world that His Word will never be destroyed. I think that's the real miracle, that God's Word was not destroyed that day, it was stronger than steel."

Veterans of the foundry were amazed. Sam Piccolo said, "The whole thing had to be a miracle. At least ten of these people should have never made it out of there without having their legs burned off, or killed." Several years earlier, a similar accident occurred. Oldtimers recalled that the spillage severely burned ten men. This time no one received a scratch.

The men took the charred remains of the shoe, the hardhat, and the untouched Bible, and encased them in glass. This display was set up in the chapel as a perpetual reminder of the day.

The accident happened on Friday. Wayne was out of town meeting with Senator Taft, executives of Lordstown, and other leaders of the industrial and political arena of Ohio. Word of Pittron's amazing turnaround had already spread to provoke interest in this neighboring state, and the men were meeting in Canton to discuss the Value of the Person Concept. The meeting was interrupted by a phone call to Wayne, informing him of the fire at Pittron.

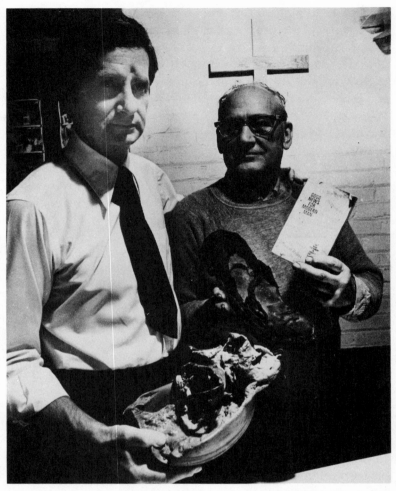

George Protz, with Wayne, holds Bible that remained untouched after a devastating explosion and a fire that destroyed everything else in its path.

Wayne returned to Pittsburgh at once, and went immediately to the plant. He was stunned by the scene of devastation. He couldn't believe the men were safe. Sam Piccolo came to him excitedly, using words like "miracle" to describe what had happened. The men had asked Sam for a special service of thanksgiving in the chapel, even though the regular meeting was not scheduled until the following Wednesday.

On Monday the men returned to work. They pitched in together to clean up the rubble left by the fire, and made the bay area operational again. They made plans for a special service to be held the next day. On Tuesday nearly three hundred men, from both labor and management, crowded the chapel to offer thanks to God for sparing those caught in the molten blaze. It was an emotional scene, and one which served to strengthen the bond that was growing between the former adversaries.

News of Pittron's "miracle" was splashed across the Pittsburgh papers, bringing attention to the foundry and what was developing there.

I. W. Abel was curious about all the stories he was hearing about Pittron. He summoned Lefty Scumaci to his office and said, "Remember that fellow you sent to me about settling Pittron's strike? What's he really doing over there in Glassport? What's this 'chapel' all about?"

He instructed Scumaci to go to Pittron to "check it out." He was to report his findings back to Abel. Lefty had no idea that this assignment would bring lasting changes to his life.

Lefty—christened Francis John Scumaci—was born on July 28, 1928 in Stowe Township near McKees Rocks, Pennsylvania. His first memories of life were the bleakness of the Great Depression. Growing up during the Depression was tough enough anywhere; in McKees Rocks growing up was tough even during periods of great prosperity.

Though situated beyond the steel valley of the Monongahela River, downstream from the confluence that creates the Ohio, McKees Rocks is strikingly similar to the old steel towns around Pittsburgh. The year 1928 was pre-renaissance Pittsburgh; it still justly deserved the epithet "Smoky City." But if Pittsburgh was dirty, McKees Rocks was filthy. It was the kind of town that moved Theodore Dreiser to his literary descriptions of plebeian life that was more pathetic than tragic. In this crucible of economic survival, Lefty learned early Dreiser's maxim that "Humanly speaking, life is a god-damned stinking game."

Lefty was a baby during the Hoover era. These were the days of the street corner apple peddler, of "Legs" Diamond and Winnie Ruth Judd, a time when holidays were something only banks were taking. He grew up hearing about CCC and the WPA as the New Deal pushed its efforts to blot out the memories of American "Hoovervilles." Babe Ruth was fading and Lou Gehrig was dying, as the nation, preoccupied with economic recovery, was moving toward a day of infamy in December of 1941. But long before General Douglas McArthur ever said, "I shall return," Lefty had heard of him as the swaggering "management bully" who had crushed the members of the marching veterans who made up the Bonus Expeditionary Force of 1932.

Lefty's father, Ross Scumaci, was one of the lucky ones. He had a job and was able to eke out a living for his family working as a rigger. Ross married the former Theresa Gidaro, who bore him five children, the eldest of whom was Lefty. The Scumaci's were a tightly knit family that kept alive the old world traditions, fiercely proud of their Italian ancestry. They were not initiates in the Society of the Black Hand, but every Italian home in McKees Rocks felt the strength of its presence. The Scumaci children learned to speak the names of the local kingpins of Cosa Nostra with respect. The Mafia was a fact of life, a force to be reckoned with, which provoked ambivalent feelings of ethnic admiration and horrible revulsion.

Francis was born with a congenital defect, a partially withered right arm. It was necessary for him to master early the art of compensation. Ross Scumaci refused to allow his son to be babied and encouraged him to develop the left arm to do the work of two. Francis did everything left-handed and the nickname "Lefty" was unavoidable. The birth defect at least made it possible for him to be called something other than Francis.

The name "Francis" may not be as provocative as Johnny Cash's "Sue," but it was a definite liability for a boy living in McKees Rocks.

The Scumaci's were deeply involved in the affairs of the Roman Catholic Church. As a youth, Lefty served as an altar boy at the Mother of Sorrows parish. He took his sacerdotal duties seriously, but always opted for the early mass. The late service found the enterprising lad violating Pennsylvania's Sunday Blue Laws on the front steps of the church. There, equipped with his homemade shoe-shine box, Lefty was hustling shines from his Sunday morning patrons.

Lefty was in high school during World War II. Nature had not only left him with a deficient right arm, but was cruel in another way to a young boy whose life revolved around sports. Were it not for the fact that he already had one nickname, the next option would undoubtedly have been "Shorty." Standing in football cleats, and drawing himself to full stature, Lefty couldn't top five feet five inches. He had the kind of physical makeup ideally suited for team mascots. But he couldn't settle for that, and used his agility and speed as weapons of compensation. While still a freshman he earned a letter on the varsity football squad, delighting the fans with his one-armed catches as an end. He played football and baseball for four years, earning the respect of his peers and his coaches for his competitive moxie.

After graduation, Lefty traveled to Chapel Hill, North Carolina, with stars in his eyes. These were the days of glory for North Carolina, which rose to national prominence on the shoulders of its greatest star, Charlie "Choo Choo" Justice. Lefty dreamed of playing football for the Tar Heels. After one week of practice, however, Lefty had to face the finite limits of his compensatory skills. It was clear that desire and heart were not enough for a short, handicapped boy to make it at a large university. With his dream of college football in ashes, Lefty went back home.

But there was still baseball, where physical size was not such a necessary prerequisite. Pee Wee Reese and Phil Rizzuto were already blazing a trail for undersized ballplayers. Lefty's sandlot exploits drew the attention of major league scouts, and he signed a modest contract with the Boston Red Sox to play with the Miami Marlins of the Florida Citrus League. This was triple-A baseball, only one step removed from Fenway Park.

Baseball in the minor leagues became a love affair for Lefty. He didn't mind the endless bus rides, the meager meal allowances, or the foul-smelling facilities that passed for locker rooms. His skills were improving with the impetus provided by keen competition, and he was moving rapidly toward the big time. As a hitter, Lefty's handicap became a blessing. Since it was almost impossible for him to stretch his arms outside the strike zone, he was forced to become selective with his swing. Thus he avoided "chasing bad balls," the bane of so many rookies. With a controlled and level swing, he proved to be a consistent hitter, spraying the ball to all fields with a high average.

It all ended abruptly when a call came from McKees Rocks informing Lefty that his father was stricken with a serious and incapacitating disease. Ross Scumaci could no longer work, and Lefty was summoned home. A minor league baseball player's salary was not enough to keep the Scumaci family solvent. The luxury of a career in sports had to be abandoned.

Lefty had no trade skills and only one week of higher education. To make ends meet for the family he had to secure two jobs. In the day he punished his shoulder laboring as a hod-carrier for a brick layer; at night he worked in a delicatessen. He was finished with sports; his dreams of Fenway Park were shattered and he was living out Dreiser's "stinking game."

In July of 1950, Lefty applied for a job at the huge and sprawling new industrial complex run by the Continental Can Company. Ross Scumaci was still coaching his son from the wings, encouraging Lefty from his sick bed. "Son, take the job. You can make something of yourself there if you have the guts to stick it out."

Within three months Lefty's father was dead, but he left his son a legacy of words of encouragement. For more than a decade Lefty worked at the factory, married to the monotonous daily routine of the assembly line. He mastered the intricacies involved in beating the quota system, thriving on the internal competition that characterizes the American factory scene. The Continental Can Company was spearheading a booming industry. Suddenly, it seemed as if everything in the world was being packaged in throwaway cans. There were beer cans, frozen juice cans, battery fluid cans, gasoline cans . . . cans for everything liquid or concentrated were being mass produced by the can industry.

Lefty did show guts, and he did stick it out. His interest, however, was always greater in people than in making cans. He observed the human element of the workplace closely. He became savvy in the different styles of corporate and union leadership, and he didn't always like what he saw. At times the internal politics of the factory were ruthlessly brutal.

The factory was a melting pot of the laboring class. Hard women worked there, whose language made seasoned veterans of the street blush; some men called the plant "America's largest whorehouse." Lefty met people inside who worked eight hours a day with glazed eyes, people made torpid by the endless repetition of the same menial tasks. He talked to people who had worked every day for ten years seated on a stool before a large container of nickle-sized pieces of cork used for liners in bottle caps. Working with both hands at once, these "corkers" became adept at pushing the cork liners into metal caps by the thousands each day. This was their contribution to American culture. Some such workers became hostile and belligerent, while others retreated into a shell of quiet indifference. Lefty met them and befriended them.

On one occasion, Scumaci spoke to the president of his local union concerning the matter of a routine grievance. He mildly questioned his leader on a recent decision. The local president sneered at Lefty, "If you don't like it, then why don't you do something about it, Dago?"

Lefty did. He answered the president's insult by running against him in the next election, winning easily. The man had obviously offended a great many others by treating them as he had Lefty. In the heat of the campaign for election, Lefty acquired a personal knowledge of the internecine warfare that went on within the union ranks.

Scumaci was president of the local union for fourteen years. His tenure was maintained largely by virtue of the trust people had in him. He was approachable, exhibiting a warmth and compassion that enhanced the organizational and administrative skills he possessed. Lefty's sanguine way with people did not escape the notice of the International Office of the United Steelworkers. In 1967 he was elevated to the level of international staff representative and given the title of wage technician. As wage technician he was a vital cog in the operation of the union, in charge of policing job descriptions, classifications, and pay scales. But aside from his formal responsibilities, Lefty distinguished himself as an ambassador of peace, a diplomat for the union. This image came slowly; it took several years for Lefty to mellow. His toughness had left a wake of trouble behind him. Over the years he was fired or suspended nine times and had been a leader in thirty wildcat strikes.

Francis Scumaci has a political sixth sense. His interests range from local union elections all the way to national presidential elections. He crossed all party lines, and soon became known by political hopefuls as a man who had extraordinary savvy. He helped organize the Kennedy Campaign in Pittsburgh, and was invited to the White House by Nixon, Ford, and Carter.

During the Nixon-McGovern campaign, Scumaci hooked up with White House staffer Charles Colson in an effort to keep the USWA noncommittal. Historically, the USWA had been strongly allied with the Democratic Party, but McGovern's platform had provoked grave doubts within the union. On a campaign trip to New York, Lefty found a hastily scrawled note in his box in the hotel lobby. It read simply, "The President of the United States called you and will call back later."

Lefty laughed with the desk clerk about the practical joke. But at 7:30 P.M. Richard Nixon was on the line congratulating Lefty for his work and issuing him an invitation to a special dinner at the White House. In the same breath, he announced that he had chosen Lefty's eldest son, Ross, to make a seconding speech for Nixon at the Republican National Convention.

Lefty's first formal dinner at the White House was an intimidating experience. He was briefed on White House protocol and entered the dining room mentally checking a list in his head about matters of proper etiquette. To appear relaxed, he lit his best contraband Havana cigar and joined in pre-dinner small talk with the other guests. As the ash on the end of the cigar grew precariously long, Lefty panicked inside. There were no ashtrays in sight and Lefty couldn't very well dispose of the ashes in his pants cuff. The alert hostess spotted Lefty's uneasiness and surreptitiously nodded toward the tiny ornate silver containers that graced the table. Lefty, noticeably relieved to discover these frail replicas of Federalist hardware were actually ashtrays, snuffed out the cigar and blurted, "Geez, I didn't know these were ashtrays. I thought I was supposed to put my nuts in there."

For half a second his words hung in the air as the sophisticates around him sought desperately to retain their social balance. It was a losing battle as with one voice they exploded and laughter at Lefty's double entendre. Far from being mortified, Lefty felt suddenly at ease as he joined in laughter at himself, an ability that has helped him to break down many social barriers.

During the early days of the Carter Campaign, the Georgia Governor was considered a dark horse. Carter knew that organized labor would be crucial to his nomination, and he also knew that Hubert Humphrey was the "darling" of labor. So Carter planned a campaign visit to Pittsburgh where the AFL-CIO was holding a convention in a Pittsburgh hotel. Carter's first stop was the convention hall. His reception there would be vitally important to his presidential aspirations. He was heartily booed. Carter was stunned by this reaction, and tried to fall back and regroup. His area campaign manager, Tim Kraft, paid a visit to Lefty and entreated him to have labor take a second glance at Jimmy Carter. Kraft was trying hard to reverse the negative reaction Carter was experiencing and said, "The Governor needs help. Is there anything you could do?"

Lefty replied, "Bring him to the Homestead Gate."

Homestead had great symbolic significance. It was the site of the famous "Battle of the Barges" in 1892 between striking steelworkers and three hundred Pinkerton men hired by Henry Clay Frick, and of the notable visit of Russia's Premier Kruschev during the Eisenhower presidency. Carter went to the gate. There, by Scumaci's arrangement, he met and made friends with Babe Fernandez, the local union president. This sparked a new relationship for Carter with organized labor. His drive toward the Presidency was greatly enhanced when he captured the key Pennsylvania primary. Carter didn't forget, and invited Lefty to his inauguration. In 1979, President Carter gave Lefty a special invitation to the White House to meet Pope John Paul II during the Pontiff's visit to the United States.

Scumaci was a man for the people, with interests in a wide variety of activities, including national involvement with the Sons of Columbus. His love and sensitivity for the working man found its managerial counterpart in Wayne Alderson. It was inevitable that their paths would converge.

Lefty visited Pittron to fulfill the instructions given by Abel. He went on a Wednesday and observed the "chapel meeting." He knew enough about Alderson and Piccolo to be suspicious. He had heard the words of bitterness spoken during the strike. What he found there dispelled his suspicions. He returned the following week, and the week after that. He made his report to Abel, but kept on going to Pittron. Something happened to him in that place: Lefty Scumaci met Christ.

Lefty's conversion did not go unnoticed back at union headquarters. He soon acquired a new nickname, "Friar Tuck." But Lefty was too well liked to become an object of ridicule. His colleagues respected him and supported his newly discovered faith.

Francis "Lefty" Scumaci, Wayne T. Alderson, Sam Piccolo (l. to r.).

In the time that followed, Lefty became close to Wayne and Sam. The two union bosses became Alderson's closest friends.

The impact of the chapel was felt not only by the employees of Pittron and visitors to the plant, it made its way into the town of Glassport. The citizens became aware of the changes in their major industrial site. They took notice when the plant was brightened by a fresh coat of paint. Stories of what was happening inside circulated around town. The wives of the workers talked about the changes in their husbands, exchanging anecdotes as they spoke with each other in the supermarket and at the beauty parlor. Pittron tales became the order of the day at church socials and community bridge clubs. Women took time to write letters to the management to thank them, saying that their husbands did not come home angry and frustrated as before.

After the fire, one of the men came to Wayne and asked if he could make a set of praying hands out of a mold. The man, John Yanderly, wanted the praying hands to be the unofficial logo of Pittron. He gave the first set to Wayne and had ten thousand duplicates made. On Easter, every employee received a ham and a molded set of the hands. They were treasured by the men. More sets were ordered by family members and friends. They served as bookends, shelf adornments, and desk pieces. More than one worker or family member had them placed in their coffins to accompany them on their last journey.

The hands were everywhere. They symbolized not only prayer, but the spirit of teamwork that had taken over Pittron. Huge paintings of the symbol were put over the three gates that marked the entrances to the foundry. Visitors were startled when their approach to the plant was met by the sight of praying hands—this was not the ordinary logo one expected to see at a steel foundry.

Glassport bought a new fire truck. On its side, in large letters, was printed *GLASSPORT—HOME OF PITTRON.* Pittron now had a new image. Instead of being referred to as a "God-damned" place it became known as a "God-blessed" place.

One more symbol forced its way into the foundry. An empty chair adorned the conference room where labor and management met. The chair was for God, His invisible presence indicated by the visible chair. At first Piccolo laughed about it, but later he was the first to guard it against any accidental use by visitors.

A labor-management contingent approached Wayne and asked permission to hold a special service of gratitude in the chapel. The group was led by Sam Piccolo and Jim Goebel. They wanted both labor and management to have the opportunity of joining together to thank God for bringing true labor peace and stability to Pittron. Wayne OK'd the idea and the service was scheduled for Sunday, January 20, 1974. The meeting was set for two o'clock in the afternoon, so as not to conflict with regular church services. The employees and their families were invited. Almost two thousand people attended the event as Alderson led them in a service of gratitude. It was exactly one year to the day after the strike had ended. For most, it was the first time the men's families had ever seen where they worked.

The men had been concerned that mid-January weather might discourage people from coming to the chapel-under-the-open-hearth. But January 20, 1974 saw the temperature rise to an unheard of seventy degrees. Even the weather was smiling on Pittron.

After the special service of thanks, the symbolic value of the chapel was established. Its worth to the men was so apparent that further challenges to its validity evaporated. Now the chapel was accepted as an integral part of Operation Turnaround.

As the winter of 1974 surrendered to the new springtime, Operation Turnaround was in high gear. It was no longer an experiment, but an established way of life within the plant. Its reputation was spreading, and Pittron was suddenly gaining industry-wide recognition.

Recognition also came to Wayne Alderson. Not only did the press notice the remarkable changes at Pittron, but other plant owners and board chairmen had their eyes on the scene. One morning, a man who identified himself as the president of a large midwestern based multi-national steel corporation called Wayne on the phone. He said that he was in town with his chairman of the board, and they wanted to meet Alderson over lunch. Wayne had never met these men before, but he recognized their names immediately. His interest was piqued, but his schedule left no room for a long lunch. Wayne politely declined the invitation, but the man pressed for a meeting.

"It's very urgent that we speak to you. May we come over to your office now for a short meeting?"

Wayne agreed and invited them over. When they were seated in the office, the chairman shut the door and spoke rapidly in quick, hushed tones.

"We need an Operation Turnaround at our plant, and you're the man to do it. We came here to talk business."

They did talk business, skipping the niceties and getting right to the point. They layed out before Wayne the plans of a manager's dream. Wayne felt like a superstar, being lured to the top with golden promises. The offer was spelled out in detail, including a salary in six figures and a five year "no cut" contract. The deal was sweetened by a guaranteed piece of the action involving a cut of the profits. It was the proverbial "offer you can't refuse." The chairman had a contract in his pocket. He put it in front of Wayne and said, "When can you start?"

"Never," Wayne answered directly. "I'm staying here. Thank you very much."

The chairman was aghast, obviously shaken by Wayne's stubborn refusal to take the bait.

"But why? Don't you like the deal?"

Wayne responded, "Two reasons. First of all, because I'm committed to these men here to finish what we started. Second, because all you talked to me about was money. You never mentioned people, and that's what I'm about."

Wayne's manner made it clear that he was serious. The men retreated from his office and he never heard from them again.

In June, Pittron celebrated its Seventy-fifth Anniversary by hosting a three-day conference on the Value of the Person in industry. Seven thousand people attended the event. Representatives from management and labor, friends, and neighbors of Pittron all gathered for the occasion, while the Communist Party picketed outside the gates, charging that the Value of the Persons program was a new management ploy to exploit the workers.

Dignitaries from the world of industry and government spoke glowingly of the hope for the future that was symbolized by Pittron's dramatic turnaround. Donald C. Burnham, Chairman of Westinghouse Electric Corporation came to the chapel and addressed the crowd.

"I don't think my presence is strange at all. I feel right at home here. I don't think it's important whether you have paneling around the room and plush seats. I didn't come to see the walls and pictures, I came down here because of the people. The reason religion and industry are compatible is that religion teaches you how to treat your neighbor. We are beginning to realize that how you treat the person in industry is important."

Labor was represented by Joseph Odorcich, then director for District 15 of the USWA. Joe Odorcich, proud of his Croation ancestry, personifies the mythic hero of all steelworkers, Joe Magarac. What Paul Bunyan is to lumberjacks, Magarac symbolizes to the men of the open hearth. Odorcich portrays the image in real life. Lying about his age, he entered the coal fields at fourteen. His youth was one of unbridled anger, which he expressed with his fists. Odorcich was thrown in jail after he put two foremen in the hospital, battering them with his bare knuckles. Bail was posted for him personally by Philip Murray, and Odorcich switched employment from the coal mines to the steel mill. But his temper got him in trouble again, and he was involved in another bloody brawl. This time Odorcich was not only fired, he was blackballed from the union. Trying for months to break back into the rank and file, Odorcich met uniform resistance. Sleeping in an alley all night, penniless and hungry, he made a vigil at Murray's office door until finally he was admitted. Murray spared no words as he gave the impetuous young fighter the tongue-lashing of his life.

"Until you learn to fight with your brain instead of your fists, you are going nowhere. Now go back to the mill, I'll get your card back. But this is the last time I bail you out."

Odorcich kept his fists in his pocket and rose to the position first of union president at Pittron and eventually to vice-president of the entire USWA. A confirmed realist and outspoken agnostic, Odorcich has little time for religion. His repeated digs at Alderson usually include the challenge, "Are you trying to convert me?"

Odorcich may struggle with God, but he is a believer in the Value of the Person and he trusts Wayne Alderson. Whatever his religious attitudes are, he has given strong support, respect, and encouragement to Alderson's work. "What you are doing is good. I respect you because I know you'll never be a quitter and I know you're not controlled by anyone."

At the anniversary celebration, his remarks were direct and credible: "I worked in that place. I knew it when it was dusty, dirty, and filthy. I was just another number. It looks like now, finally, somebody is recognizing that these are people. Treat the people decently and the work you will get out of them will be a hundredfold more than if you high-pressure them. These people are special. They know how to work. They will work and work hard if you treat them like human beings."

At the anniversary celebration, Operation Turnaround was on display. The men were eager to give their endorsement to what had transpired. They spoke in glowing terms of hope that what happened there could be duplicated elsewhere.

Piccolo commented on the ripples of reaction that were spreading across the nation. "We have received telegrams and letters from Canada, California, Florida, New York, Japan . . . you name it, we have them. It can happen any place people have guts . . . people who will try it and a management team willing to lead it."

The anniversary celebration was a milestone for Pittron and for Wayne Alderson. The attention given to what was happening in Glassport made it clear to Wayne that the Value of the Person concept was something men and women everywhere were yearning for. A raw nerve had been touched, and those in pain started looking to Alderson for healing balm and a new kind of leadership.

Operation Turnaround rode its crest for twenty-one months.

Its future looked bright. But the dark clouds on the horizon were coming closer, gathering momentum as they approached. It was the lull before the storm. A corporate grenade was ticking menacingly at Alderson's feet.

# 6

## The Penalty for Overachievement

Near the end of the summer of 1974, rumors began circulating around Pittsburgh that Pittron, in the midst of phenomenal growth and prosperity, was about to be sold. At first not much stock was put in these rumors, but they refused to die and the speculation grew intense.

It was August, and Wayne was on vacation from Pittron. This was the year the Alderson family took the trip that spanned not only the Atlantic Ocean, but bridged the thirty-year gap between World War II and the present. His family was going to see the places that they had envisioned as they heard Wayne speak of the war, and of Red.

Alderson, in three decades, had not forgotten the misery of his first crossing, which found him violently seasick from the moment his troop ship sailed past the Statue of Liberty on its way out of New York harbor. No more ships for him—this time he went by air.

The plane touched down in Brussels. Clearing customs, the family rented a car and began to retrace Wayne's earlier route with the Third Infantry Division. Step by step they followed the path of the American invasion that had ended abruptly for Wayne in the front trench of the Siegfried Line.

They visited the villages and towns the GIs had liberated, speaking with people who still remembered the spring of '45. Frenchmen who had been children at the time spoke excitedly of their memories of American tanks driving in triumph with hatches open as soldiers tossed candy to the flag-waving children. The older people spoke more softly of their memories, speaking of sons who had fallen for France and of the grim determination of the Resistance to keep the hopes of liberation alive.

Bullet-scarred buildings were still in evidence. Monuments and special stones marked the spots where acts of heroism had taken place. Wayne found buildings still standing where he once flushed Germans from their posts. A rustic wooden watering trough, with its rickety sides, patched and sealed over, was still flowing with the crystal cold water Wayne once used to cool his canteen. He remembered fondly milking a vagrant cow and filling his canteen with milk, milk that was savored because it was the first he'd had since reaching the front. The landmarks brought it all back, far more vividly than Wayne thought possible. He recalled the monuments that had stood there in 1945. There, in the interior of France, was a memorial not to Frenchmen but to German soldiers who fell in combat during the early days of the Nazi invasion. Four huge pillars elevated iron crosses, inscribed with the words, "Wir sind für den Führer und das Vaterland gefallen."

The family drove across the border into Germany. Showing their papers at the checkpoint, they were greeted by a friendly guard who wished them a pleasant visit. The irony of the contrast struck Wayne. He was not alone, crossing a creek in the dead of night listening intently for enemy movement. He was now in an air-conditioned car, riding in comfort with his family.

The signpost announced *ZWEIBRÜCKEN—2 KM:* they were approaching the edge of what had once been the Siegfried

Line. They stopped and spoke to the villagers who emerged from their houses to see the strangers. One of the oldtimers proudly hailed his English-speaking son, who volunteered his services as a guide for the Aldersons. The ruggedly handsome German had been only six years old when the American's achieved their costly breakthrough on the way to Berlin. He still remembered the childhood fears he'd had during the battle. Time had not erased the memory of two of his playmates who had been killed as they were caught in the midst of a man's war. He spoke of these things as he escorted the Alderson family to the infamous site.

The view that greeted Wayne was startling, not at all what he expected. There were no immediately visible remains of the hideous dragon's teeth. In their place was a rolling stretch of farmland. He looked out over wheat fields, rhythmically swaying in the summer breeze. The atmosphere was tranquil, denying the facts of history. The land itself seemed calm and docile, totally at peace with its inhabitants. It reminded Wayne of a pastoral scene in Nebraska, of "amber waves of grain."

The family stood for a moment at the edge of the forest that had served as the staging area for the jump-off on that fateful day in March. They began to walk slowly across the open field where Wayne had raced madly nearly three decades before. There were no land mines this time; no machine gun bullets flying through the air. Yet Wayne's legs were trembling as the awful memories of that place took hold of him. Unnatural blemishes in the terrain before them grabbed their attention. Large bushes growing in the middle of the wheat field seemed out of place. The guide explained that they were especially planted to conceal the ruins of the Siegfried fortress that would not yield to attempts to excavate them. The teeth of the dragon had been pulled, but their concrete roots were still intact, impacted in the earth that once had been burrowed with the tunnels of war.

One eyesore marred the landscape. The German command pillbox that took such a heavy toll on the charging Americans was still standing there defiantly. Wayne scrambled up on the pillbox and gazed back across the field, trying to imagine what it must have been like for the Germans who manned it that day.

In his imagination he became a German soldier, nerves wracked from enduring a night of relentless shelling. He could see the armada of American tanks poised for attack on the edge of the woods. He envisioned wave after wave of enemy soldiers racing toward him across the fields, signaling the start of the allied juggernaut. From that side of the dragon the Siegfried Line did not feel impregnable. It was an eerie experience.

Wayne jumped down from the concrete bunker and started walking with careful deliberation. Just days before, his family had walked the field where Billy Weaver was killed by a skimmer. They had walked through the town where Joe Stankowski was slaughtered by German armor. Now he approached the spot where he and Red had stood locked in a final embrace of death. This was holy ground. Like a biblical patriarch, Wayne wanted to mark the spot with an altar of stones. The site was burned indelibly into Wayne's soul, but there was no external sign to mark it, no inscription or plaque. The only visible mark was the indentation on Alderson's forehead—a modern mark of Cain to remind him of his debt to Red. His flesh was crawling as the sharpness of his memory made him almost feel Red's arms around him as he slid to the ground in death. He stood there choking back tears. It was at this place where one man died and another was left to live. Here was the real birthplace of the Value of the Person.

Nancy and Nancy Jean watched Wayne as he stood riveted to the spot, lost in time. Now they could understand what made Wayne a driven man.

The Aldersons left that place with no desire to go back. For Wayne, the past was now behind him. They drove in silence back to their hotel in town. This was more than enough for one day, but the day wasn't over yet. When they entered the rural hotel, the old fashioned lobby was filled with people buzzing with excitement. As night fell, small groups were gathering in front of a television set as news of an important international broadcast was heralded.

Wayne sat down on the only vacant section of a faded sofa in the lobby. When he glanced at the man seated beside him, he suddenly realized why the seat had been vacant. The man was horribly disfigured, grotesque. His right eye and ear were missing, and a jagged scar ran from the base of his neck up and across his face. The left side of his face was normal, but the right side was a mass of scar tissue. He was German.

The two men began to make small talk. The German spoke English well and asked Wayne about his background. Wayne briefly recounted the odyssey he had just completed with his family. When he spoke of Red and the Siegfried Line, the German's eyes began to mist and his lips started to quiver. It was difficult for him to speak, but finally, with great effort, the words came out.

"I was there. I was in that trench. . . ."

As he spoke, it was obvious that he was caught up in his memories, fixing his eyes on the phantoms in his mind.

"You Americans wouldn't stop . . . you just kept coming. There was no place for us to run."

Wayne could not believe it. He was sitting next to a man who had been severely wounded that same March day, shot in the face by a charging American soldier. This was "the enemy." The scene was emotional as the men embraced each other while thirty years of frustration poured out. Today they were comrades, weeping over the futility of the ultimate expression of the politics of confrontation. The war was fought by men like these—the rank and file of the military; it did not belong to the generals alone. It went far beyond the Eisenhowers, Pattons, Montgomerys, and Rommels of that era. It belonged to Allied and Axis boys who now were reaching mature manhood, boys like Wayne and his new friend. They sat together welded into friendship, mourning the past as the television set came on and the President of the United States announced his resignation to the world.

The next day the Alderson family journeyed to St. Avold. With the visit to Red's gravesite, the pilgrimage was complete. Wayne audibly said goodbye to Red, and started to leave the cemetery. On the way back to the car, Wayne noticed a name on a grave marker he passed. The name jumped out at him: *STANKOWSKI, JOSEPH.*

"It couldn't be," Wayne said to Nancy. "I'm sure Joe's remains were shipped back to the States. It must be a different Stankowski."

Wayne and the women walked quickly to the office. A clerk dusted off an old register and started scanning the names. It was there. *Stankowski, Joseph Pfc.—Canonsburg, Pa.* They returned to the gravesite and took pictures. Wayne would carry the photos back to America—to Canonsburg, where the Stankowski family could treasure them as their final keepsake.

Emotionally drained, Wayne returned to the French hotel, where the family made preparations for their return to America. The phone rang with a transatlantic call for Wayne. Bud Hyduk, Wayne's assistant, was on the other end. With a note of urgency in his voice Bud said, "Wayne, you have to come home. Rumors are running wild here that the plant is being sold. The men are all deeply concerned. You'd better get back here fast."

Wayne hung up and looked wistfully at Nancy.

"Oh, for real bullets again," he sighed.

"What do you mean? What's wrong?" Nancy asked.

Wayne explained the phone call to his wife. "At least in the war I knew real bullets were flying around. You could hear them and see the tracers. At least you knew when to duck. In the corporate wars the bullets are invisible and silent. I don't know what these rumors mean, Nance, but they could mean trouble."

The Aldersons flew out the next morning. There was no more time to indulge in memories.

On the flight across the Atlantic, Wayne and Nancy discussed the possible personal complications of a buy-out. The brass from

central headquarters had already been dropping
Operation Turnaround was making them nervous. A
news article on the chapel had circulated through the
corporate offices, provoking questions and not a few jokes about
Pittron turning into a "Sunday School." Wayne understood that
new ownership often "cleaned house" of old management, re-
placing the executives with men trained in their own systems,
policies, and leadership style. He wondered aloud what new
ownership would do with Operation Turnaround, the chapel,
the men, and him. Only time would tell.

Nancy cautioned Wayne, "Don't do anything rash. Whatever
happens you have to think of the men. Sam has said all along
that the men are better off with you than without you. The men
would surely understand if you slowed down a bit."

There had been talk of making Wayne the next president of
the division, but the carrot had been dangled in front of Wayne
with a "hidden" condition that was not so well concealed. The
price of the presidency would be to maintain a low profile with
the "religious thing," and to cool off his involvement with the
rank and file.

Ironically, Wayne had recently led a Bible discussion about
the Apostle Peter. He was "the rock"—the bold one who made
public confession of Christ. He was a trusted member of Jesus'
inner circle of disciples. Yet it was Peter who urged Jesus not
to go to Jerusalem. It was Peter who urged Jesus to play it safe.
Wayne had no visions of grandeur about himself. There was no
"messiah complex" taking root in his psyche. But he and the
men had discussed the fact that every Christian faces those
moments of decision in life where one must choose whether to
"go to Jerusalem" or stay home in bed. So often courage is
beaten down by the advice of well-meaning but overly protective friends and loved ones.

"Don't say that, Nancy. Sure my friends want to protect me.
You don't want me to get hurt. But don't you see I have to be
who I am? I can't compromise that."

Wayne wanted to do what his friends and family suggested,

but an inner compulsion made it virtually impossible. It would be like fleeing the point. A part of him knew that if he retreated now, his friends would hate him later. Temptation was coming from the people he loved. Alderson was headed for a private Gethsemane. He prayed earnestly that God would let him back off. Wayne didn't hear any voices from heaven, but God's answer was clear.

Wayne was at work the next day. He talked to his management team, and to Pittron's president. The answers he received made it clear that there was substance to the rumors. Textron was in serious negotiations with an out-of-state concern that was making strong overtures to buy Pittron.

Wayne was concerned. He sought to buoy up his own confidence by telling himself he would not be a casualty. He had a track record that would vindicate him in the event of any criticism.

He could still see G. William Miller's face when he promised Wayne he would judge him by results. He could envision the set jaw, the furrowed forehead, and the look of sincerity in his eyes when Miller announced, "There will never be a penalty for overachievement." There was no reason for Wayne to doubt him. *That's my safeguard,* thought Wayne. *He meant what he said. The bottom line will protect me.*

Wayne thought the matter over and conceived a bold plan to keep Pittron together. In a daring move, he approached the officials of Textron and asked permission to buy the plant personally. He made a desperate offer, promising to put up a substantial amount of "hand money" immediately. The conditions were simple: he asked for ninety days to raise the necessary additional funds to purchase the foundry. He agreed that if he failed to raise the money, he would forfeit the down payment. He had no idea how he would ever be able to do it, but he was willing to take a long shot.

The offer was refused. It was obviously too late. The prior negotiations for the sale of Pittron were well beyond the talking stage; the contract was ready to be signed. Textron's chairman already had his exquisite gold pen in his hand. He was a businessman who knew the fundamental law of profits; buy low, sell high. He had found a high bidder. Pittron was being sold to Bucyrus-Erie, makers of the world's largest strip-mining and earth-moving cranes. Two years earlier, it would have been difficult for Textron to give the foundry away—it was about to close the deal for a sum of nearly eighteen million dollars.

In October, an officer of Textron informed Wayne that executives from Bucyrus-Erie would be visiting the plant in a few days to consummate the deal. Wayne was alarmed.

"I hope they don't come on Wednesday. I would hate for this to interfere with the chapel time that means so much to the men."

Alderson was given full verbal assurance that the meetings would not interrupt the chapel. But the next Tuesday afternoon, the same officer poked his head in the door of Wayne's office and announced, "The Bucyrus-Erie people are coming tomorrow."

Wayne shot up out of his chair, protesting.

"Don't get excited. Sit down. I told you not to worry. The meeting will not be scheduled to conflict with the men's chapel time."

Wayne calmed down and sat back in his chair, but he still wasn't convinced.

The next morning, Alderson went to work feeling apprehensive. His intuition was working overtime. He was hearing the tinny sound again. In his gut he had the feeling that he was being set up.

No word came for a meeting. The longer the morning dragged, the more anxious Wayne became. His palms were moist as he waited in his office for word. Alderson was transformed into a "clock-watcher." He watched the second hand on the wall clock sweep around the dial. With each revolution, the knot in Wayne's stomach grew tighter. It was like waiting for jump-off.

At 10:45 A.M. Wayne pushed his chair away, got up, and started the long walk to the chapel-under-the-open-hearth. He felt certain that he was making the walk for the last time.

As he walked, he was gripped by the same foreboding he had felt long ago in Germany. The plant seemed unnaturally quiet. His concentration was so intense it was as if no one else was in the building. His mind was playing tricks again. It was like night patrol, his legs were moving but he was standing still.

He began to move, taking in every detail of the plant along the way: the fresh cleanliness of the foundry floor, the acrid aroma of the molten steel. His eyes marked each fish on the steel beams, guiding the way to the catacombs below. On the final ramp he stopped. He stood there for a moment thinking of the first day he saw the spider-infested storeroom. So many changes had taken place, first in the room and then—most importantly—in the men.

Getting a grip on himself, Wayne finished his walk down the ramp. Electricity was in the air surrounding the men who waited at the chapel entrance. There were hundreds of them, no one wanted to miss this day. They had to know if Wayne was going to show up.

Alderson greeted them casually, giving no outward sign that anything was wrong. He moved to the front of the chapel, arranging his open Bible at the makeshift lectern as he waited for the men to settle in their benches. At 10:58, a messenger rushed into the chapel bringing a note from the management offices upstairs.

"You are summoned to a meeting at 11:00," it read. A wave of shock and fury swept through Wayne. The words signaled an act of total betrayal. He saw the runner as a Judas-goat bearing tidings of perfidy. Wayne's reply was curt and abrupt.

"Tell them I will be up as soon as the Bible discussion here is over."

The men heard the exchange. No one spoke. They just looked at Wayne with fascination, as if they were watching a suicide victim leap hundreds of feet to his death.

Minutes later, the messenger was back. This time his message had the tone of an ultimatum.

"You must come. Now! All management staff is required to be at the meeting."

The tension in the air was explosive. Wayne's teammates from management looked to him for a decision. The set of their faces made it clear that they were ready for a signal to stand by Wayne. By now this was their own program, not merely the fancy of one individual. Wayne spoke to them decisively.

"Go to the meeting, I'll be up in a few minutes."

Reluctantly, the management team left the chapel and went upstairs. Wayne stood there watching, as one by one the white hats vanished from the room. He loved those men deeply. They had joined him in taking serious risks for the sake of a new management style. The last thing he wanted to do was to drag them down with him.

While Wayne began the opening prayer below the open hearth, upstairs Pittron was being sold.

Wayne tried to keep the Bible discussion on its normal course. The chapel time was not a time for discussing company business. That was understood to be out of bounds. His efforts on this day, however, were futile. No one wanted to talk about the Bible yet. Finally, one of the workers broke the silence. He raised his hand and asked the question that was in everyone's mind.

"Is Pittron sold?"

Wayne looked at him as if to say, "You know that kind of question is out of order." As one body the men stared back, not accepting Wayne's dismissal of the question. They all wanted to know, and their eyes told Wayne the answer had to be given.

Wayne spat out his one word answer. "Yes."

No one spoke, but the men's bitter disappointment registered on their faces. Some looked down at their feet. Others stared blankly ahead. Wayne's eyes fell upon Deacon Lunsford, who was sitting in the front row. Deacon didn't move. His face revealed nothing of what he was feeling inside. But Wayne saw the almost imperceptible movement of Deacon's hand. He was holding a Bible on his lap, squeezing it with all of his might, turning his brownskinned knuckles pale white. Deacon lived by the Book. Now he was clutching it as his last straw of hope.

Wayne tried to rally the men, knowing their mood was growing more explosive. He tried to give a pep talk, like an industrial Vince Lombardi inspiring his players at half-time. The words came with difficulty as Wayne reminded them of the past and of what had been accomplished. He pleaded with them not to go back to the old ways. He spoke of the obstacles that had been overcome, of the new spirit of teamwork that had emerged. He reminded them of the racial barriers that had been demolished, of the hatred that had evaporated. He spoke in urgent tones.

"Today you are very close to changing the industrial world, where a person lives and works and becomes a human being. Don't throw it away. You are so close to victory, and so close to defeat. If you react the wrong way now you will put this place right back where it was. The only people who can destroy what we've built together are the people sitting right here. We are the ones who could put it back."

He was interrupted by another question.

"In your honest opinion, do you think you will be here to help finish the job you started?"

Wayne didn't get a chance to answer the question. Before he could say a word, another man jumped up, purple with rage, furiously shouting to anyone who would listen.

"Do you want me to answer that? No! I've got news for you. I don't care what dump bought this hole. I don't care what anybody thinks. That man standing there is a man. Now there ain't nobody here got nothin!"

Somebody reached over to calm him down. He threw the arm aside yelling, "Get away from me before I smack you in the mouth."

He knocked over his chair and stormed from the chapel.

Wayne said quickly, "You can't do that, you can't go back to dog-eat-dog. I'm not indispensable. If you men put your faith in me you're dead wrong. If you do that you've missed the whole point of what's been going on in this room for months. Think beyond me. Think of your families, of the other plants that are starting to follow your lead. Think of the God who is working here in your midst."

The lunch hour was coming to a close, and the machines in the foundry were waiting to be manned. But no one wanted to leave. Everyone sensed that they were facing more than the end of a meeting. It was the end of a dream, and of a treasured relationship. They couldn't just say, "See you later," and go about the routine work of the plant. Instead, as one body, the men rose and pressed to the front of the chapel. They gripped each other's hands in a human chain linking each man together in a bond of prayer. Alderson prayed aloud in halting tones as muted sobs were heard here and there across the room.

As Wayne ended his prayer the men broke hands, stood awkwardly for a moment, and then began to shuffle silently out of the room heading for cranes and chipping molds.

Lefty Scumaci and Sam Piccolo waited behind. They approached Wayne with grim faces. Sam put his hand on Wayne's shoulder and said softly, but clearly, "You better get up there fast."

Wayne left the chapel quickly, moving up the ramp with rapid strides. When he got to the conference room nobody was there. He was too late, the meeting was over.

Wayne walked straight to the parking lot though it was only noon. He climbed in his car and drove out the gates of Pittron. The car seemed to be driving itself as he was caught up in his own thoughts. Cars passed him by, but he didn't notice them. The stops and starts at traffic lights were performed automatically, as if a robot were at the wheel. He was stunned, numb to the world around him. The corporate grenade had exploded in his face. His car was like a stretcher carrying him from the front lines to safety, and he wanted to get home. He wanted Nancy. Yet he was not looking forward to telling her what had happened.

His conscience accused him with painful stabs. He had defied authority. He was known to be stubborn and at times uncommonly brash, but he always stopped short of defiance. Never in his days as a soldier or his tenure in the world of industry had Wayne Alderson ever disobeyed or openly defied an order. Disobeying orders ran counter to his beliefs. But he had done it today. There was no denying it. He had openly and publicly defied a direct order from his superior officers.

He understood fully what that would mean. In wartime such an action could result in a courtmartial. He could be shot. In industry there was no firing squad, but an industrial "court-martial" was inevitable.

In his confusion, Wayne sought to justify his action. They had betrayed him. They had promised the meeting would not interrupt the chapel. But these rationalizations didn't work. He knew very well that management had the prerogative to change its mind.

Wayne wasn't sure in his own mind why he had done what he had. *On the one hand,* he thought, *I didn't want to disappoint the men. On the other hand, maybe it was a matter of pride, a question of losing face with the workers.* The deeper he probed his conscience the clearer the answer was coming. *I could not compromise. I had to do what I knew was the right thing.* He smiled for a second to himself as he recalled the words of Davey Crockett: "Be sure you're right, then go ahead." Wayne was sure he was right. Whatever the motivation, one thing was absolutely certain to him: the die had been cast.

As soon as Wayne walked into the house, Nancy knew something was very wrong. Not only could she read it on her husband's ashen face, but he was home earlier than usual. Too early.

"What happened?" she asked softly.

Wayne poured out his story. Nancy listened in silence. There were no recriminations, no "I told you so's." Without words, Nancy communicated that it was all right. They embraced for a moment and held each other without speaking. Finally Nancy said, "It had to be. . . ."

Dinner was eaten quietly that evening, as neither of the Aldersons had much of an appetite. Wayne picked at his food as he pondered the questions of their future. He was still hoping that something would happen to make things right again.

About eight o'clock the door bell rang. Wayne rose slowly to answer it, momentarily annoyed by the intrusion. He didn't want to be disturbed; he wanted to be allowed to think in peace. He opened the door. Standing there was the president of Pittron. Wayne invited him in.

His visitor got to the point quickly.

"We have a revolt on our hands. I would like you to come in tomorrow morning and meet with the people. After you left, the men were ready to rebel."

He told Wayne that Pittron was faced with an unusual possibility: the threat of a wildcat strike led not by the union leaders or the rank and file, but by the management team. Wayne's management allies, led by Bud Hyduk, were threatening to close the plant. They were furious.

Wayne hesitated.

"What's my status if I do come in?"

The president spoke straight.

"You don't have a job anymore, Wayne. You're finished. You're too close to the men. You're emotionally involved. I told you this would happen. We've been sold; it's over. Please come in and talk to the men."

The boss left, and Wayne's hopes went with him. He respected the president and admired him deeply for coming to his home like this. He knew it must have been painful for him. They were friends, and the president had backed Operation Turnaround again and again.

Wayne went to bed early, but sleep eluded him. His mood kept switching from anger to remorse. He thought, "I'm fired. I'll close the plant. The men will follow me." The idea of revenge was all too sweet. But then he thought back to the words he himself had spoken that very morning in the chapel. He couldn't allow his feelings to destroy what they had all worked so hard to achieve.

The next morning, Alderson returned to Glassport. His memory was jogged back to the day after the strike was over. Now there was no exciting challenge to stimulate his interest; he was returning in limbo.

He went to the machine shop where the management team was gathered for the meeting. They were poised for action, just waiting for the signal to hit the bricks. A question was shouted out.

"Mr. Alderson, are you fired?"

Wayne ducked it slightly. "I don't know. My future is in the hands of Bucyrus-Erie."

Another man cried, "Lead us out of here."

Calmly, Wayne answered, "I can't do that. I can't preach one thing and practice something else."

Wayne rejected a management-led work stoppage. He called them to peace. A management strike would mean reverting to the same policy of confrontation they had worked so hard to overcome. It would contradict everything the Value of the Person stood for. The management team knew it, but they couldn't stand being in a position of helplessness. They had stood with Wayne shoulder to shoulder in the past. They wanted to stand with him now. But Wayne's talk of peace quieted their angry reactions.

Alderson spoke a few more words of encouragement, then left his friends to go to his office and perform the ignominious task of cleaning out his desk.

Sam Piccolo and Lefty Scumaci were not willing to accept Alderson's dismissal. They couldn't believe that Eugene Berg, Chairman of Bucyrus-Erie, would ever fire Wayne if he knew all the facts. Sam and Lefty drafted a committee of representatives from the labor force at Pittron, and went *en masse* to Wayne's home. They urged him to make sure that he was, in fact, fired. They pleaded with Wayne to contact Berg. To satisfy them, Wayne went to the phone and put in a long distance call to Milwaukee.

With the men standing around, Wayne said, "Mr. Berg, I have been told that I no longer have a job, but no one from Bucyrus-Erie has given me that message officially. There are many rumors and much confusion here, and I would like to know exactly what my status is."

Chairman Berg responded by saying that the decision was not yet final. He invited Alderson to come to Milwaukee where the two could meet to discuss Wayne's future.

"When do you want to see me?"

"Tomorrow morning," Berg replied.

Sam, Lefty, and the men standing around the phone were delirious. In the tumult of their joy they were positive that the "misunderstanding" would be soon rectified and sober reason would prevail. Wayne stared at them in bewilderment. He looked at the matter coldly, considering it from a management perspective. The handwriting was not yet erased from the wall, and their jubilation was premature. Yet the phone call did offer Wayne one more slim chance.

Early the next morning Wayne flew out of Greater Pittsburgh Airport. As the airplane lifted off the runway and soared skyward, so did Wayne's hopes. He thought to himself, *Surely the chairman is an intelligent man. He will certainly see the value of what's been accomplished in the twenty-one months of Operation Turnaround. He'll judge me by the results. He will understand the bottom line.*

The plane touched down smoothly in Milwaukee. The entire flight had been pleasant—a good omen, he thought. Alderson made his way to Bucyrus-Erie's headquarters, his confidence growing steadily. Now Berg would be dealing with Alderson in the flesh, not with the rumors or legends hiding beneath the surface of newspaper copy.

When Wayne entered the executive offices he was greeted personally and warmly by Mr. Berg. Another good sign. He was obviously not going to be subjected to a corporate runaround, or be kept waiting in an outer office.

When Wayne set eyes on Eugene Berg he was taken aback by his appearance. Tall and lanky, Berg was a throwback to another era—he was a hard, two-fisted man who had fought his way to the top. Wayne liked him immediately.

Berg gave Alderson the kind of treatment usually reserved for top-level executive prospects being wooed on a job interview. The meeting lasted all day and proceeded congenially, spiced frequently with frankness. The men understood each other.

"I want to thank you for the opportunity that is now ours to buy one of the most successful foundries in the world," Berg said warmly. "We consider you to be one of the most brilliant managers we've ever seen. I'm impressed by Pittron's financial statement. I know that if it weren't for you, there would be no foundry to buy. But your management style is different from ours and we have some problems with it."

Berg skated over the insubordination incident, making it clear that it was not the real issue. He emphasized that he was not opposed to the men having a chapel where they could meet on their own time. With him, religion was not an issue. His concern was with management walking with labor. Bucyrus-Erie had company-wide management policies that couldn't be changed overnight to accommodate an innovative style. Berg spoke candidly.

"Wayne, I think what you are doing is a good thing. The world needs it. But we're not quite ready for it yet. I'm afraid you're a little bit ahead of the times. Would you be willing to give up your involvement with the men and the chapel-under-the-open-hearth? The men would still be free to meet there on their own time, but I want you to get out of it."

Before Wayne could form a reply, the chairman put the question to him again in a way that could not be evaded: "Will you give it up?"

For Wayne, this was the moment of truth. The last chance he had to retain the job he cherished was suspended in front of him. He felt the full weight of the question. He sensed that his integrity would stand or fall with his answer. Compromise was at least feasible. If he said "yes," he would be able to continue as an influence in the plant. Operation Turnaround could be carried further towards its maximum potential. *Perhaps* he thought, *I could carry on the Value of the Person concept outside the plant—on neutral turf where no one would be threatened.*

Wayne's lips began to form an answer. His mouth was open, ready to say "yes," but what came out was "No sir, I will not give it up."

Wayne stood on the far shore of his private Rubicon. Berg gazed at him sadly and repeated that his company was simply not ready to follow Alderson's style.

"Well, Wayne, if you cannot give it up then you no longer have a job. The choice has been yours."

It was clear to Wayne that Berg did not relish the verdict. It was obvious that the conclusion was agonizing to him. Wayne couldn't help but admire the character Eugene Berg displayed in making the toughest of all management decisions.

As is frequently the case in moments of tension, comic relief was necessary. Wayne laughed out loud and said, "How could I be so good and still get fired?"

On the return flight to Pittsburgh, Wayne tried to imagine what it would be like to be unemployed. He was now a statistic, a casualty of the corporate wars. But he was not overcome with gloom. His spirits were lifted by the realization that the decision he had been so frightened to make was now behind him. The moment had come and gone; it had seemed almost easy.

When Wayne arrived home, he saw Lefty's car in the driveway. *Faithful Lefty,* he mused. *He's always around when the chips are down.* Lefty had made a special trip to be there when Wayne returned. When Wayne walked in the door, he glanced at Lefty and then spoke directly to his wife.

"I made a friend today, Nancy."

"But you lost your job," she replied knowingly.

Wayne said, "Yes," as Nancy's eyes revealed a look of compassion.

Wayne turned his attention to Lefty, who sat in the chair chewing his cigar, shoulders drooping. Most infants don't begin to speak until they're at least a year old. Lefty Scumaci was born talking. But on this occasion he didn't know what to say. He felt that words would be useless, and listened in silence as Wayne recounted his conversation with Berg.

When Wayne finished the story, he picked up the phone and called Sam. Piccolo responded to the news in stunned disbelief. To him the verdict meant that Operation Turnaround was over.

Wayne was left to face the public's reaction to his firing. Alderson's public image was crumbling. Wayne was crushed with disappointment, but he felt no shame. His work at Pittron had attracted widespread public attention, and the news of his dismissal was also a public matter, and the news media were attracted to the story. John Moody of the *Post Gazette* called Wayne and asked for an interview. The interview culminated in a feature story leading off the second section of the paper, dated February 10, 1975. The bold headlines proclaimed, *EXEC WHO CHAMPIONED BIBLE CLASS AT GLASSPORT FOUNDRY OUT OF JOB*

He did feel a measure of embarrassment as the news of his dismissal was aired in the press. He noticed the funny glances people gave him on the sidewalk. He tried to help people who stumbled awkwardly with their speech as they tried to express their condolences. All of a sudden, it was as if he were walking around with his head shaved again. He soon realized that in our society, when a man loses his job, he also loses his identity. He began to feel like a pariah.

The most painful consequence of the firing occurred the next Sunday morning in Church. Wayne and Nancy held their heads high as they entered the sanctuary to join the congregation in worship, as they had done regularly for twenty-one years. They were not prepared for what happened during the morning announcements. The minister stood up and informed the congregation that Wayne had been fired. He went on to say that he had prepared copies of the news article and made them available for distribution at the back of the church.

Nancy couldn't believe it was happening. She felt that her husband was being made a public spectacle. The announcement hurt her deeply, and an awkward atmosphere fell over the congregation.

Why was the announcement made? Was it motivated by the pastor's compassion, in an effort to call upon the people to support the Alderson family during their crisis? Was it an attempt to humiliate a layman who dared to intrude into the domain of the clergy? One fact is clear. Whatever the motive, the Aldersons interpreted the act as a judgment upon them. Yet they realized they could be oversensitive at that moment. They also knew it would be out of character for their minister to behave in a spiteful way. He had demonstrated on many occasions that he was, indeed, a man of compassion.

Wayne and Nancy left the church deeply hurt and shaken. Wayne recalled the angry words of America's most famous militant atheist, Madelyn Murray O'Hare. "The Christian Church has the only army in the world that shoots its wounded."

In the days that followed, members of the Alderson's Christian fellowship groups made no contact. Wayne inferred from the silence of his friends that he had become an embarrassment to them. He felt like a person left alone in a cancer ward, shunned by those who were afraid of his disease. The family was confident that they could deal with the specter of unemployment, but were not sure if some of their friends could. However, they determined not to leave their church or their community. They loved both too much for that. This was their home. The church had been a focal point of their married life. This was the place their only child, Nancy Jean, had been baptized and confirmed.

Wayne was the first casualty of Pittron's management team, but he was by no means the last. In the weeks and months to come, the men who had walked with Wayne were "retired" or dismissed one by one. The honor roll built steadily. Pittron's sales manager lasted three months. The production manager went in six months. A few lasted a year or two, but most were quickly fired. All of them paid the price for their loyalty to Operation Turnaround and the Value of the Person. They were the unsung heroes of Pittron.

Changes in the union-management relationship were quick in coming. The rank and file kept the chapel going, but it was boycotted by the new management force. The politics of confrontation were brought back. Piccolo reported to the press that seven grievances were filed in the first eight weeks following Alderson's dismissal. Sam Piccolo's office was taken away, and he returned to seeing his men in the cab of his crane.

The men tried to keep peace, but disappointment ate away at their morale. Piccolo confirmed that just before Alderson was fired, the union was on the verge of signing a six-year labor agreement. The signing was planned for January 20, 1975, the second anniversary of the end of the eighty-four day strike. Alderson had once promised the men that as long as the Value of the Person was in effect there would be no strikes. There would be no need for them. They believed him and were busy preparing the contract.

Piccolo told the news media that the six-year pact would have ensured years of peace, security, and labor stability. But with Alderson out, Sam said he would not be interested in signing a long-term contract with the new management.

"In fact," Piccolo was quoted, "There could be difficulty agreeing on even a short-term contract."

Somehow, the agreement was made and a strike was averted, as the men clung tenaciously to the gains they had made. But by July, twenty-one months and three days later, tension came to a head. A wildcat strike erupted when 750 men walked out of the plant. The official issue centered on the firm's withholding vacation and holiday pay for about fifty workers. The walk-out lasted seven days. When the men returned, sixteen of them were charged with inciting an illegal strike and were fired. Ten of them were fined by a federal judge for violating his order to end the walkout. Sam Piccolo was not fined—he was fired.

Piccolo filed a petition with the National Labor Relations Board. He waited outside the plant for nine months before his case was heard. The rank and file had lost both their management and union leaders. During this time, Piccolo was interviewed on a television talk show. He said, "If this would have happened to me before Operation Turnaround, I would have burned down the place. Now I'm committed to a different style. I will abide peacefully with the decision of the Board. It's in God's hands."

Piccolo won his case. The verdict favored the union, and Bucyrus-Erie was ordered to restore Piccolo to his job.

The old Pittron is gone, but the Value of the Person is still alive at the foundry. The chapel continues to this day, led by the rank and file. Some of the workers have since retired, others drifted away. But many persist, convinced that what they experienced was real and worth struggling to maintain. They look for a better day, when reconciliation will replace confrontation as the accepted method of labor-management relations.

For Wayne Alderson, life had to go on. But he had learned one cold and brutal lesson: G. William Miller was wrong. There was, after all, a penalty for overachievement.

# 7

# Have Film–Will Travel

Wayne and Nancy Alderson were left to reassemble the pieces of their lives, which had, like so many parts to different jig-saw puzzles, been strewn chaotically on the floor. Nothing seemed to fit together, no clear pattern was visible. An old question still hounded Wayne: *Where is God in all this?* It didn't make sense. Why had God spared his life in the war? Why had he traveled to the threshold of death and returned? Why had God awakened him in the middle of the night? Was this all part of a vast eternal plan, or was Wayne the butt of some cruel cosmic joke? Wayne had come off the reservation, sticking his neck out for God, only to have it chopped off. Wayne was beginning to feel what is described as "the dark night of the soul." He wrestled daily with these questions, at times clinging to faith by his fingernails.

One of his greatest fears involved what his firing would do to other people. He was afraid that his example would discourage them from taking risks of faith in the work world. People needed to be encouraged, not intimidated. Wayne saw himself as a point man for God, called to inspire other people to follow his lead. To be a Christian in a secular world requires boldness. But when the leader falls, the faint of heart often flee in terror. What purpose could possibly be served by having Operation Turnaround seriously wounded when it was on the brink of total victory?

Wayne didn't regard the Value of the Person as a mere management program. He saw it as a pulsating movement that could eventually change the battle-scarred face of industry. His vision was bigger than Pittron: he wanted to see sweeping reform in the whole scope of labor-management relations, everywhere. He was utterly convinced that America, indeed the world, could not survive on a constant diet of confrontation. It would take strong leadership and high visibility for the Value of the Person to become a movement and get the attention of the masses. Wayne knew that the people wanted it; they were longing for the restoration of their dignity. But now the only example he seemed to be able to offer was an example of failure.

Wayne realized that people would be saying, "Look what happened to Alderson. He tried to be different, but he got shot down." The pessimists would be singing songs with lyrics that cried, "You can't beat the system." The unwritten rule that God and business don't mix would be set in concrete. The vultures would be picking his bones clean, and the cynics would be gleefully saying their favorite words, "I told you so."

Outwardly, Wayne appeared placid and unflappable. But on the inside his emotions were churning like a spiritual cement mixer. His visceral reaction was to question the very wisdom of God. How could God be identified with failure? Wayne had heard enough cliches and pat answers to these questions to last him a lifetime. He was weary of all the "stiff upper lip" advice he was hearing. He was a Christian, not a Stoic. He needed reassurance and, once again, he leaned on Nancy, who never wavered from her deep inner conviction that God was right in all He did.

Nancy didn't need to see how all the pieces fit together. Her faith was simple and solid. She trusted the hidden counsel of

God. She lived by the daily maxim that God was with them, and His will, though at times painful, was never capricious. God did not waste the experiences of people. She was sure there was an unseen plan to all this. Nor did Nancy lose faith in her husband. She was not a Job's wife who said, "curse God and die." Nancy's faith in her husband was a dogma, fixed in her mind from the day she met him. From the Halloween party to the Duquesne incline, from the Veteran's Hospital to St. Avold, Nancy Alderson had a growing conviction that God had touched her man in a special way. She saw his clay feet every day, and marriage to him was at times difficult, yet she remained unshakable in her conviction that she was wed to a man of destiny. That destiny could never be aborted by his firing. There had to be more to it.

In Nancy's eyes, Wayne had not been "fired"; rather, he had been "released" by God for a more important mission. Wayne was not being mustered out with a dishonorable discharge; he was being transfered to a new front, he would be assigned to a new point in the same war. Nancy didn't believe for a moment that Wayne's dismissal was orchestrated merely by Bucyrus-Erie. She saw it as God's work, removing Wayne from a job he loved and would be content to keep till he died, so that he could move on to a higher calling. Nancy believed there was truth in what the management manuals said—that dismissal is potentially a springboard to bigger and better things. Bucyrus-Erie had closed one door, God would open a new one. Nancy's theme song in all this was a Christianized version of *Que Sera, Sera,*—what will be, will be.

On the other hand, Wayne had moments when he was tempted to quit. He had had enough wounds for one lifetime. He thought of retreating to the reservation, but he knew he would die there. If he quit now, he would lose his own dignity. He had to keep going. He didn't know where and he didn't know how; he wasn't sure if he even knew why. But he knew one thing, he had to keep going. He could be fired, but he would never quit. He hung on to some words he remembered from a

Hollywood war movie, "Retreat, hell! We're just attacking in a different direction."

Wayne remembered his own first principle from the early days of Operation Turnaround: "give . . . expecting nothing in return." Once again it was put up or shut up.

Wayne didn't shut up. If the advocates of management by confrontation thought they were rid of Alderson, they were in for a surprise. Hindsight would make them long for the old days when Wayne was "contained" at Pittron. He was fired, but by no means silent; he had lost his job, but not his tongue. The man with a hole in his head was about to take on an even greater dimension of boldness.

At first, life slowed to a walk. The bustling pace that had been a part of Wayne's routine was temporarily tranquilized. For the first time in years, Wayne had time on his hands. He used this time to regroup, spending hours searching the Bible for answers to his questions. In that search he discovered some things about himself and about the ways of God.

Wayne was a manager. His youth may have been shaped by the coal fields, but his adult life was shaped by the corporation. He had become a member of a different order. He knew all about firing people. It was never a task he relished, but he knew the rules of the game and had come to accept playing by them. At times a manager's life was like that of an athletic coach as "cut day" approached. He knew decisions to cut aspiring players or to fire failing employees could have a devastating effect on the lives of the victims. Firing is brutal, no matter how gently it's done. Euphemisms were usually employed in futile attempts to minimize the sting. Men weren't "fired," they were simply "not retained," "given early retirement," or "let go."

The business school text books gave instructions on how it was to be done. They warned against the torturous process of firing a man in stages by subjecting him to successive demotions, reducing him to a helpless beggar. A "clean break" was the method espoused by most experts. The rationale was simple. To retain an incompetent employee, or one whose presence was disruptive, was to harm both the company and the individual. Firing becomes necessary to ensure the general welfare. The person who was fired benefited by being released from a no-win situation, gaining a fresh opportunity to find more suitable employment elsewhere. Dismissals should be clean and—if possible—amicable. Those are the rules of the game.

Wayne Alderson had understood all that when he was doing the firing—but now he had to apply those principles to himself. He didn't kid himself with the hopes of future reinstatement with Bucyrus-Erie. He knew there was no such thing as an amicable divorce.

In his search through the Bible, he discovered a few things about God and failure. He learned that <u>God's ways are not only mysterious, but at times downright absurd</u>. Why, for example, had God encouraged the patriarch Jacob to migrate to Egypt for relief from a famine? Surely God knew that a future Pharaoh would exploit that opportunity to enslave the whole people of Israel and reduce them to a very lucrative free labor force. But Pharaoh hadn't heard of Moses yet. . . .

Why did God allow the Apostle Paul to have his missionary activity thwarted in the midst of the most successful growth period of the Church's history? Thrown in jail, all Paul was able to do was sit around and write letters. The same Apostle once found it necessary to "fire" one of his team, a young man named Mark, who went home and wrote a Gospel. Indeed, God had allowed His own Son to die at the hands of vicious men, an act which, ironically, made redemption possible for them.

Examples were multiplied. They hit Wayne full force as he read them. <u>He became aware that God is not absent from suffering—He lives in it.</u> Wayne began to see what the corrupt peddlers of the gospel of easy grace try so hard to conceal from their converts. The way to God is the *via dolorosa,* the way of grief. Wayne paid the price of the cost of discipleship. His religious life echoed a principle he had learned in business years earlier, "There's no such thing as a free lunch."

Further discoveries in God's school were a bit rough on his

ego. He had related easily to New Testament calls to "bearing fruit," equating fruit-bearing with productivity. Surely God couldn't quarrel with Wayne's bottom line. Wayne wanted God to judge him on results. But Wayne soon discovered that God valued some things even more than "success." The Deity's priority sheet listed obedience far ahead of success. Wayne couldn't earn a "merit increase" in the Kingdom of God.

Finally, Alderson learned a lesson that eludes many Christian leaders: no man is indispensable to God's operation. In God's army, just like in Patton's or MacArthur's, all point men are expendable. Operation Turnaround belonged to God, not to Wayne Alderson.

Wayne was left with two pieces of his puzzle intact: his faith and his family. By some strange quirk of alliteration, he was provided with a third "f", which would prove to be the key to further expansion of the Value of the Person movement. It was a film.

The film came about through an odd set of circumstances. Back in 1974, filmmaker Robin Miller was in Pittsburgh producing a documentary about productivity, absenteeism, alcoholism, and related labor-management conflicts. In the course of his research, he spoke with frustrated churchmen who were weary with efforts of applying evangelical band-aids to Fortune 500 problems. One of these men was aware of what was happening at Pittron, and made it his business to get Alderson and Miller together.

The men met on the first day of Pittron's Seventy-Fifth Anniversary celebration. Miller arrived, one of many strangers who attended the event, and Wayne assigned one of his men to give Miller a guided tour of the plant.

"As I made my way around," Miller recalls, "observing the environment and talking with the rank and file, I came to the initial conclusion that what I was witnessing was based on only two possibilities. Either this was all a carefully contrived and executed PR gimmick and everybody from the ad agency to the grievance committee was in on it, or it was real.

"By the 3 P.M. shift change, I had my answer. I had bumped into everyone from the local union president to college kids working for the summer. I knew five hundred more names, faces, and handshakes than I did seven hours earlier. I was tired ... but I was happy. I can't say there wasn't a dissenting vote, but it was clearly a landslide. These men knew they had something very special and they were vocal about it. I saw a good story, too good not to tell."

Miller squeezed in meeting time with Alderson during the celebration, and they agreed on a program to create a documentary film on Pittron. Miller's rules were clear. He was concerned that what was happening be authentic. No script would be written and no professional actors employed. The script would emerge from taped interviews of the men and women, allowing the dialogue to be spontaneous. Only the fire would be recreated; everything else would be filmed as it happened.

"Perhaps most important," says Miller, "I needed the freedom to create the film on behalf of a public audience. It could not be controlled in any way by Textron, its sponsors, or even Wayne. . . . A story too good to be true would only be believed if it *were* true and honestly told on film."

Production began immediately. In the weeks that followed, slices of daily life in the foundry were transposed into color and sound: the meticulous carving of wooden patterns by the patternmakers; critical molding in sand of giant steel castings; selection and melting of high alloy steels; highly orchestrated pours with two and three ladels of steel to make one 400,000 pound part; x-raying for defects; air-arcing and grinding out defects; all the heat, dirt, noise, and sweat of the men of the foundry at work. Then the contrast of the chapel-under-the-open-hearth. Forty hours of film were shot, processed, printed, and recorded. Then came the monumental months of editing together three picture tracks and seven sound tracks for the hour-long feature documentary.

A special premiere of the documentary was scheduled in Glassport on October 27, 1975, almost a year to the day after Alderson's dismissal. The film was still untitled. Together, Robin and Wayne brainstormed possible titles. They considered calling it *The Value of the Person, The Pittron Story,* or *Operation Turnaround.* They scrapped all these and finally settled on *Miracle at Pittron,* to highlight the dynamic events surrounding the fire. But at the last minute, Miller had a flash of insight and said to Wayne, "To me, it seems there is a bigger miracle than the fire. Why not *Miracle* of *Pittron?*"

Wayne instantly agreed, and the film was titled just as the announcements were being sent out for the premiere. Letters were sent to a few employees of what was now called Bucyrus-Erie, inviting them and their families to the showing. The mayor of Glassport and other community leaders were invited. Special invitations were sent to G. William Miller and Eugene Berg, but they did not respond.

On Sunday afternoon, nearly two thousand people jammed into a school auditorium two blocks from the foundry to view the premiere. Sam Piccolo and Lefty Scumaci stood on the stage, proudly making introductions to the assembled crowd. The lights were turned out and the film began. The film was starkly realistic. The men of Pittron sat in the audience transfixed by the vision unfolding before them. They saw themselves swinging sledge hammers, operating cranes, pouring steel, and sitting in the chapel. All the memories of the days of Operation Turnaround were rekindled as they watched themselves in action on the silver screen. Viewers were at times distracted by the audible weeping in the room.

When the film ended, the auditorium was shaken with a raucous standing ovation. People started shouting for Wayne, who was watching it all happen from an obscure niche in the back of the hall. As the men shouted for him to come forward, Wayne moved quickly, the adrenaline flowing within him as he mounted the platform. These were his people, the ones that counted. It was like a homecoming celebration. As he spoke to the crowd he was soberly aware that for this brief moment, one year after being fired, he was reunited with his men.

Before the premiere there had been one showing of the film. It was screened privately to a select audience in the Oval Office of the President of the United States. Those who were with Gerald R. Ford testified that the President had been moved to tears by what he had seen. On the day of the premiere, Wayne received a telegram from the White House.

017007 005 DLY GOV'T WHITE HOUSE DC 10-25 NFT
PMS MR. WAYNE T. ALDERSON, DLR DONT DWR
52 DUTCH LANE                    1975 OCT 27 AM 100
PITTSBURGH, PA 15236
DEAR WAYNE:
YOU HAVE MY BEST WISHES IN THIS PREMIERE SHOWING OF THE MIRACLE OF PITTRON, A FILM ABOUT WHAT MEN CAN DO WHEN THEY HAVE FAITH IN GOD AND FAITH IN THEMSELVES. IT IS MY HOPE THAT YOUR EFFORTS AND THE EFFORTS OF THE STEEL WORKERS OF THE MON VALLEY WILL SET AN EXAMPLE FOR THE FUTURE OF LABOR-MANAGEMENT RELATIONS IN AMERICA.
SINCERELY,
GERALD R. FORD

The President was genuinely interested in Pittron because it offered a clear alternative to the methods found elsewhere, which were rapidly bringing the nation to the brink of economic disaster. Here was a model that he could point to as a paradigm for the kind of effort needed for his "Whip Inflation Now" campaign.

The President was not the only person touched by the film. During its production, some of Miller's production crew were also touched. They couldn't help violating a cardinal rule of documentary filmmaking—not to get personally involved. They were working people too, a cross-section of ethnic, religious, and non-religious backgrounds.

"My wife, my staff, and I will never forget this," Miller said later. "We who lived it, even briefly, have been touched. We can never go back. I was the man beside the camera at the last chapel who was in the way of the angry worker who left. I was the one he threatened to 'smack in the mouth.' "

As the film was being completed, Alderson had to make some decisions about his career. He didn't look for a new position in industry, or send out resumes. He simply didn't have time. From the day he was fired he was inundated with requests to speak at churches, campuses, business and labor seminars, and the like. There was no room on his calendar for "full-time" employment. A new vocation was being thrust upon him from without. He was becoming "public property," a catalyst for raising the consciousness of the industrial world to the importance of valuing people.

With the documentary finished, Wayne had a model to show the world. He had his evidence in celluloid that the Value of the Person concept could and did work. People might argue with his theories, but they couldn't very well argue with the evidence they saw on the screen. The film became his chief credential.

Wayne became a special labor and management consultant, a job that thrust him into the role of peacemaker. Like an industrial Johnny Appleseed, Wayne began criss-crossing the country, living out of suitcases, rushing to catch planes, showing the film, and "spreading seeds." Sometimes he was paid for his services, many times he was not. When the calls came he went to a labor seminar in Michigan, a church meeting in Ohio, a management pow-wow in Texas. Soon he was having trouble keeping up with the multitude of requests that kept flooding in. His program was obviously touching a vital nerve, as the nation awakened to serious internal problems in the work world that were not being solved by traditional methods.

It was a grueling schedule, but he was refreshed and encouraged by the response of so many people. He especially enjoyed visiting college and university campuses, where he and the students had an easy rapport. While still at Pittron, he had spent hours with college students who were employed by the foundry during the summer months. Somehow they were able to bridge the generation gap. Perhaps it was his boyish look or his enthusiasm that captivated them; perhaps they saw in him a middle-aged man who was more idealistic than they were, who balanced his idealism with years of real experiences. The students were open, wide open, to the Value of the Person. They longed for it in their own workplace, the classroom. They knew the folly of confrontation, having grown up in the days of Vietnam and Kent State.

Eventually, Wayne was invited to show the film at Princeton University and to speak in the University Chapel. The term "chapel" was misleading to Alderson. He expected such a place would be a small, quaint wing off to the side of a larger auditorium. The word conjured up in his mind visions of the meeting place under the open hearth at Pittron. These visions perished when Wayne walked into the magnificent gothic structure Princeton so modestly refers to as a chapel. Wayne found a gorgeous edifice that stood in bold contrast to the chapel at Pittron. There were no spider webs or rats to contend with, no rough-hewn benches to test the toughest posterior. This was Princeton, where the worship of the Almighty was appropriately elegant. The people in attendance were not dressed in coveralls or grimey blue shirts, they wore today's student uniform of blue jeans and t-shirts. But the grandeur of the room and the differences in clothing didn't change the response to Wayne's words—that stayed the same as it was virtually everywhere. Students wearing loafers were as interested in love, dignity, and respect as men wearing steel-toed work shoes.

Alderson's address in the chapel was to follow an unusual format. It was to be a "dialogue sermon" in conjunction with a seasoned veteran of the pulpit, Dean Ernest Gordon. Gordon's dialogue sermons were merely a euphemism for the rugged debate format to which visiting speakers were subjected.

Dr. Gordon was a twenty-three year veteran of the Deanship.

Gray-haired, tall, and commanding, he spoke with a heavy Scottish burr. His academic erudition was intimidating and unnerving to many professional scholars who had run the gauntlet with him before. Gordon was tough, at times even brutal in his cross-examination. He was a survivor of Japanese prison camps and the author of the widely acclaimed book *Through the Valley of the Kwai.* Supporters of Alderson, sprinkled through the congregation, were apprehensive as he mounted the pulpit to square off with the Dean. The audience had seen Gordon reduce more polished speakers to inarticulate mumbling countless times. It was like Rocky taking on Apollo Creed—a rank amateur thrown in the ring with a polished professional. But Ernest Gordon had a tiger, nay, an alley cat by the tail.

Three times before the dialogue began, Alderson asked the Dean what the subject of the sermon would be. Three times he replied that it would be wide open, with no prepared notes or announced topics. Finally Wayne pressed him, "Dean, would you ever go anywhere and give a sermon like this without preparation?"

"Absolutely not," Gordon replied, grinning sardonically. Alderson was walking where angels feared to tread.

As Wayne walked up into the pulpit, he counted the steps as he went—there were exactly fourteen of them. He was thinking, *Lord, why am I here? I don't have any right to be here. I have none of the right credentials to speak in this place.*

But Alderson did not allow himself to be cowed by the Dean's strong personality. In fact, he was stimulated by it. Oblivious to the gothic surroundings, Wayne responded blow for blow, haymaker for haymaker to Gordon's verbal assault tactics. Wayne warmed to his adversary, recognizing him as a worthy opponent.

"I liked his style," Alderson said later. "He was an alley cat too. I didn't have to play games with him. He was a man who was obviously in touch with the realities of life. He was like steel, yet there was a quality of gentleness about him. He tested me severely but I sensed that he, of all people there, understood what I was about. He gave me no breaks—that was obvious, but behind it I felt a genuine sense of encouragement."

One witness who had often observed Gordon's dialogue sermons said, "What came through during the sermon was how God took over, despite Dean Gordon's efforts to take command. He's wiped out many a speaker with his infamous dialogue sermons. Wayne Alderson and John Stott, Rector of All Saints Church in London, England, were the only two men I have seen survive this format. John Stott had the power of personality, the international stature, and the experience to survive. But on that Sunday morning I was fearful Wayne would be eaten alive with words. Instead, soon the Holy Spirit was filling the place. I could feel a warm glow down in the fourth row of pews; I knew that our God triumphed."

At the end of the sermon, Wayne was escorted back to the Palmer House by his host, Arch Davis, with the encouraging sound of two thunderous standing ovations still ringing in his ears. The student response to the Value of the Person was a clear sign that Wayne was touching a nerve. This student generation, though less militant than its predecessors of the sixties, was certainly not apathetic. Wayne was starting to rouse a slumbering giant in the student world.

Wayne's escort and host at Princeton was Arch C. Davis III, Director of the John Witherspoon Institute at Princeton. Davis serves as advisor to the C. S. Lewis Society of Princeton University. Named after the famous Oxford don and late convert to Christianity, the society exists in order to promote his love of the science of apologetics—the intellectual defense of the Christian faith. Davis was overwhelmed by Alderson the man. In a personal letter to Wayne he wrote,

There is another moment I remember with equal import. We were walking back to the Palmer House where you were staying, and as you talked, I was afraid that at any moment you might throw your coat down on the sidewalk for us to walk on. Worse still, I was afraid that you might, just might, lie down and die for us right there on Nassau

Street. I have escorted a lot of famous theologians around Princeton, and have taken care of a number of fine Christians, celebrities and otherwise, but I have never quite thought that any was ready to die for me in the near future.

During none of this time had you mentioned a thing about your war experiences, or that a man died for you. This communication somehow came between the words. I was . . . the closest thing I can come up with, is, embarrassed . . . by the thought that you might lie down and die. I am a sinful man, I thought, and besides it would be scandalous right here on Nassau Street. People just don't do such things. . . . I knew all the apologetics, and I was saturated in Christian philosophy. Here I saw another aspect of Jesus the Christ. It was important for us in Princeton to see the life as well as the way and the truth. I also saw the tough gentleness of Jesus, a man who had the sort of love that can kill and the sword that brings life.

Princeton acted as a catalyst to bring the attention of the student world to the Value of the Person. In fact, a copy of the film was retained at the Princeton Theological Seminary for use in an academic case study. Shock waves went out from New Jersey to other campuses across the nation as more and more interest was being generated by the film, *Miracle of Pittron.* Interest was provoked in high schools and elementary schools as well.

Nothing excited or encouraged Alderson more than the response of a twelve-year-old boy in Lookout Mountain, Tennessee. Tad Hutcheson had seen *Miracle of Pittron* when it was shown to a group of Chattanooga businessmen in his parents living room. Tad called Wayne and told him that his friends in his sixth grade class would like to see the film. When Alderson agreed, the boy became a one-person organizing team, going to work to make it happen. He talked to teachers, the principal, and his classmates, and organized a showing for the whole school. Wayne was touched by the fan mail he received from the children of that school, he was moved by the fact that so many children could grasp ideas that eluded so many adults.

The student world embraced Wayne's vision of a work-world

reformation that added new levels to the consciousness of human dignity. Though still reeling from the disillusionment of Kent State, their youthful idealism was still alive. But it must be remembered that the students have little vested interest in the status quo, little power to lose, little prestige to be threatened. That is not the case, however, with some of their parents, grandparents, and older siblings. There are many in positions of power and authority who are very much threatened by talk of work-world reformation.

To assume that the days of the robber barons are over is to be naive in the extreme. Ruthless power-mongers are still to be found at every level of American institutional life. Wayne Alderson was an astute player in the business world; but in the arena of power politics he was a novice, a green recruit all over again. This "Johnny Appleseed" was soon to meet up with people who were not eagerly awaiting the growth of spiritual apple orchards in their fields. As Wayne traveled about, he was getting an education, meeting all kinds of people. He found men and women in leadership roles who had obviously earned their way to the top by competent achievements; he found others who had scratched and clawed their way, leaving the mangled wreckage of people whom they had used and exploited in their wake. He met some leaders who wielded their power with grace and humility, and others who were positively Machiavellian. Both types were found throughout the power structures of American institutions. He encountered them in business, in labor unions, in government, in education, and even in the hierarchy of the church.

On the other hand, Wayne met some Christian leaders who were men and women of outstanding integrity, people who were not driven madly by a lust for power or lucre. Such a man was Bill Bussiere, a tireless man who was a giver, not a taker. As a layman representing the Washington Fellowship, he worked daily with the national leadership of Canada, acquiring an international reputation for dynamic and responsible ministry. In March of 1977, he called Wayne to invite him to speak at a dinner meeting hosted by Canada's Minister of Labour. The purpose of the dinner was to bring together, for dialogue, high ranking officials from labor, management, and government.

At the request of the Labour Minister, Wayne and Lefty flew to Ottawa where they made their way to the palatial Parliament Building. There, before members of Parliament and industrial and union officials from the provinces, they showed the film and spoke about the Value of the Person. The response was enthusiastic, as Canada was at that time embroiled in serious labor disputes. The discussion, which went on until midnight, involved such keenly interested participants as Joe Clark, who would eventually wrest the office of Prime Minister from Pierre Trudeau—only to lose it to the same man a few months later.

Trudeau was not present for the meeting, but he was briefed about it by his staff and met privately the next morning with Alderson and Scumaci. He warmly embraced the Value of the Person Concept saying, "This concept could not only bring labor and management together, but it could be precisely what we in Canada need to bring our divided nation together again."

The Canadian visit also sparked an enduring friendship between Wayne and Shirley Carr. Shirley was serving in an elected position as the executive vice-president of the Canadian Labour Congress. An aggressive, no-nonsense woman, she had gained a reputation for being outspokenly critical of governments and managements that played games and used gimmicks, promising "better conditions" for workers. She knew that many of them were merely camouflaged methods of exploiting people, and she said so.

Both Wayne and Lefty braced themselves upon meeting her, expecting a verbal barrage. But they were pleasantly surprised when she turned out to be sensitive and sanguine, welcoming the Value of the Person as a sincere and genuine concept. A woman with strong principles, she discovered that she shared many of the same visions that drove Alderson. As she travels throughout Canada and the world, she uses her own talent and influence to demand human dignity for all people.

The Value of the Person movement was beginning to take on an international face. The documentary was shown in Ireland, England, Holland, Germany, and throughout free Europe. Inquiries were coming in from Japan, Australia and other parts of the globe.

As Wayne's traveling pace accelerated, his new vocation imposed new and important adjustments on Nancy. Nancy was a very private person, preferring to keep business duly separated from family life—but now she had to face the pressure of maintaining an office for Wayne in her home. The Swedish traditions were now becoming as precarious as the proverbial fiddler on the roof.

She believed the maxim that "a man's home is his castle," and Nancy had used her decorating skills and quiet dignity to provide a regal setting for her personal "king." But now the king was upsetting the castle, turning it into a frenetic nerve center of business. The castle was becoming an office complex, in which Nancy felt more like a Kelly Girl than the reigning queen. Her home, which had always been immaculate, bearing immediate witness to Nancy's eye for beauty and penchant for order, was now constantly cluttered. She had a "Johnny Appleseed" running in and out of the house, leaving his papers and scribbled phone messages strewn everywhere in disarray.

Nancy spent her time running between filing cabinets and the telephone, in a futile attempt to bring order to the chaos. She enjoyed being married to a point man, but now he was dragging her out to the point with him. But even though it meant a tremendous amount of adjustment, Nancy didn't want it any other way. She believed in what her husband was doing. If it meant she had to become a "point woman," then so be it.

Nancy had grown accustomed to Wayne's long hours away from home when he was working at Pittron, but now he was gone for days at a time, spending most of his time on the road. His trips were punctuated by brief interludes of a day or two at home. She didn't know which was worse, having him gone so much or dealing with his non-stop pace when he was home.

During the hours and days she stayed at home by herself, the telephone her only companion, Nancy had time for reflection. Between answering calls, filing information, and writing letters to Nancy Jean, who was away at Grove City College, she thought about her husband. She was enormously proud of him, but she was also worried about his future.

Her hobby was flower arranging, and her affinity with the soft and the beautiful made her recoil at Wayne's tales of violence in strikes that had become ugly. When threats were made against Wayne, Nancy shuddered, wishing at times that her husband would stop. She wistfully yearned for the return of peace and quiet to her home, for the constitutional right of all Americans, domestic tranquility. She wondered what life would be like if Wayne would take a normal job again.

Because there is so little of it, Nancy and Wayne value the time they have to be alone together. Most special are the intimate moments spent in prayer together. Nancy does not take that time for granted. She had waited too long for that part of their life to develop. It was strange—when Wayne was on the road, he would pray with anybody and everybody. He was not ashamed to bow his head in a steel mill, an executive suite, or in a coal mine. But he was embarrassed to pray with his own wife. He tried not to think about this glaring inconsistency and Nancy didn't nag him about it, until one day, while on a trip, circumstances forced Wayne to deal with his own hypocrisy.

An anxious woman approached him. Her face was contorted in pain, not from physical distress, but from obvious emotional turmoil. She asked Wayne to pray with her, and they bowed their heads together. While Wayne prayed aloud to God for the woman, she spontaneously reached over and clutched his hand, squeezing it with what seemed like a death grip. When Wayne finished the prayer, he opened his eyes and asked her directly, "Does your husband pray with you?"

"No, never," she replied tearfully.

The woman's husband was a clergyman. Her eyes were saying to Wayne, "If only my husband were like you. He's afraid to pray with me, but you're not."

Suddenly Wayne saw himself as one of the world's worst hypocrites. Here he was comforting a woman whose husband wouldn't pray with her, while he had a wife at home who was suffering the same fate. The irony of the situation was not wasted on him, and he resolved to change his ways. If he could pray with other men's wives, then he'd better start praying with his own.

When Wayne returned home, he set about the task of turning his resolution into action.

It was the most difficult thing he had ever done with his wife in twenty-five years of marriage. He was timid and embarrassed about it, and got it over with quickly. He took Nancy by the hand and led her straight to the bedroom, while she just gave him a puzzled look.

Wayne sank down to his knees at the foot of their bed while Nancy remained standing, gazing at him quizically. He looked up stonefaced at her and said, "Let's pray together, Nance."

Nancy was afraid to believe he was serious. She had hoped so strongly and waited so long for this moment that she wanted to pinch herself to make sure it was real. Saying nothing, she slowly sank to her knees beside him. If she enjoyed standing beside her man, she relished all the more kneeling beside him. They said nothing to each other. Wayne squeezed her hand, and closing his eyes, he began audibly pouring his heart out to God. The intimacy of that moment transcended all other intimacies ever shared in that room.

It was not a one-time-only exercise that would be phased out with the pressures of time. It became a regular but never routine practice. They had discovered a magic secret that the marriage manuals never mention. Wayne and Nancy consider their bedroom sacred ground, the place where they discovered a fresh kind of intimacy. Alone together in prayer, they were transported back to their own private Eden where they could be man and wife, "naked and unashamed" before the presence of God. As they knelt together, holding hands, they felt not only the presence of God, they felt love and support flowing from each to the other.

This new dimension of their marriage added sparkle to Nancy's life. It was a welcome bonus, a needed plus to sustain her during this time. The adjustments were not all easy. With her husband out of a job and her only child away at college, Nancy was left to face new challenges. One of the greatest difficulties was learning to meet these new demands without the help of one of her most important support systems. Her mother, who had been a rock for both Wayne and Nancy, was gone. The strength that woman had exuded, her constant supply of encouragement and practical wisdom, was sorely missed. A vacuum was left behind that no human being could fill.

Mother Holt died in her eightieth year. She had been ill and in the hospital many times before with rheumatoid arthritis. The crippling disease had left her with gnarled fingers and pain of which she never complained. Though her health was deteriorating sadly, her spirit was robust.

But this time it was different: her sickness was unto death. It was diagnosed that she had a fatal cancer which was progressing rapidly, sapping her of strength and eating away her life. When she had to go to the hospital for the last time, she persuaded her doctor to admit her to a large metropolitan hospital in Pittsburgh that had a unit specializing in treatment of patients suffering from terminal cancer. She loved that hospital—it was one to which she had been many times in the past for treatment of other disorders. She had always received the best of care and felt valued by the attending physicians and nurses. If she had to die in a hospital, that was where she wanted to be.

As the end came closer, however, it was apparent that the hospital had changed. Advanced technology and specialization had brought with it bureaucratic red tape and general depersonalization of patient care. Wayne was inwardly enraged as he watched his mother-in-law being treated as an object. In the throes of death, Mother Holt was suffering. She lay there with tubes coming out of her body, attached to machines. One day a tube became blocked, causing extreme pain. Wayne went out of the room to find a nurse, walking to the nurses' station to ask the woman in charge to come back to the room and fix the tube.

"I'm sorry," she said abruptly, "I'm going off duty now. You'll have to wait until somebody else comes in."

With that, the nurse turned and walked away. Wayne fought the impulse to run after her and grab her and shake her, shouting, "That woman in there is dying! Don't you care? Can't you stay five minutes to relieve her suffering?" Instead, Wayne just stood there watching the woman walk away, with the Value of the Person—and the value of the patient—going out the door with her. The need for dignity in medical care facilities as well as steel foundries was painfully obvious.

Evening came, and Mother Holt was scheduled for surgery early the next morning. Wayne kept a vigil with her long into the night. The elderly woman was failing, but remained alert. She looked at her son-in-law and said in her accent, which she had never lost, "Vayney, I'm going to die, aren't I?"

Wayne's first impulse was to deny firmly that death was near. The doctor had made no such announcement, and it would have been easy to lie. But Wayne knew about death. He sensed its irrefutable presence in the room. He looked down on her and said softly, "Mother, I can't lie to you. Yes . . . you are."

Mother Holt said nothing. She looked up at him as though she were more sorry for him than for herself. Wayne couldn't keep his tears in check as they started to slide down his face. A tear fell on Mother Holt's face, and Wayne instantly recalled that moment in France when a nurse had wept on him. Mother Holt put her gnarled hand to Wayne's cheek and wiped away the glistening drops.

"Don't cry, Vayney. I'm ready to go. I vonder how it's going to be?"

Wayne answered her question from his battlefield experience. For the first time, he told her about his own taste of death. He described it in vivid terms as the old woman listened in silence, a beatific smile covering her face. She fell peacefully asleep.

Nancy appeared in the room promptly at dawn. Preparations for surgery were made, and Mother Holt was wheeled out of the room into the hall to be transferred to the operating room. Her strength was almost gone. She tried to speak but the words were inaudible. Wayne leaned over, putting his ear to her lips. She muttered weakly, "I love you. I'm not afraid."

Wayne whispered back, "Oh, Mother . . . you look for me there. I'll be coming one of these days."

With that, the nurse wheeled her away, moving down the long corridor. There was no surgery. Mother Holt died before they reached the operating room.

After her mother was buried, Nancy thought about her daily. She remembered her not in the horror of her death, but in the spirit of her life. Somehow, she had always been able to understand Wayne in ways Nancy never penetrated. At times, she thought her mother understood him better than she did herself. Now, as so many rapid changes were intruding into her life, she wished she could talk to her mother again.

She knew what her mother would say, "Let him go, Nancy. He has to do what he's doing. Be there when he needs you, but let him go."

Nancy knew what kind of man she had married. She knew he would never leave the point.

# 8

## Coal War

It was December of 1977. The previous winter had been severe, shattering cold weather records throughout the northeast and midwest. The energy experts were fearful of a repeat performance by Mother Nature, warning that another hard winter would seriously deplete our fuel resources.

The problems encountered the year before had been hard. People in cities along the Ohio River remembered the sight of coal barges paralyzed on the river, held at a standstill in the frozen water. Those long, steel, flat-bottomed monsters were trapped helplessly by the ice mass. With the barges out of commission, the cities waiting for their cargo could only suffer meekly.

Now some forecasters were grimly predicting the onset of a new ice age. The Farmer's Almanac was pessimistic about the winter of '78. The caterpillars had an extra heavy coat of wool, and the squirrels had stashed away a spare cache of nuts. It looked like another year of heavy use of oil, natural gas, and coal.

December brought tidings that this year's crisis would not be provoked so much by nature as by people. Word was filtering out of the bituminous coal fields of Kentucky, Ohio, West Virginia, and Pennsylvania that a major strike was imminent. Wayne recognized the rumblings. His ear was to the ground and he was certain the warnings were not scare tactics or idle rumors. He knew a strike—a big strike—was coming.

Early that December Wayne had spoken at Princeton. In the University Chapel he had said, "At midnight tomorrow, December 5th, nearly two hundred thousand coal miners are going to walk out of the mines. What is our society doing to prevent it? Nothing. When the violence comes and lives are lost, utterly wasted, we will sit in our living rooms with the heat registers turned down, wringing our hands, asking ourselves how it could happen. We will be spectators watching it happen as if it were inevitable. I tell you, it is not inevitable. . . ."

Just a few days prior to his trip to Princeton, Alderson had addressed a clergy conference in Pittsburgh. Many of the participants were ministers from the outlying coal regions. They all knew a strike was coming and were intimately aware of what such strikes did to the families involved. They knew their own burdens of ministry would be multiplied as their communities would, once again, become armed camps.

It was obvious that the clergy had already chosen sides, according to the socioeconomic makeup of their individual congregations. Wayne wondered out loud, who were the sheep and who were the shepherds in these churches? He spoke to those pastors of the need of a ministry of reconciliation, a theme about which they were supposed to be experts. He urged them to be peacemakers, to transcend the divisions and lead the people in coming together for peace. He pleaded with the clergy, "We need to set our priorities straight. The people look to the church for leadership in times of crisis. We need prayer more than programs, commitment more than committees, and most emphatically, we need God more than goals. That's what the people want from you. Why don't you give it to them?"

His pleas for involvement were interrupted by a minister

who spoke with a trembling voice. A mixture of anger and pain was written on his face. The clergyman's countenance betrayed deep inner conflict, which his words confirmed.

"My son is a coal miner. If he strikes, I'm going to throw him out of the house."

Wayne was stunned as he listened to the man pour out his emotions. He recognized grief behind the anger. Wayne thought to himself, *The strike isn't on yet and already families are divided; it's like an industrial civil war.*

At midnight on December 5, the miners walked out—and with them the son of the minister. Desperate last minute efforts of mediation and negotiation were not able to avert the walkout. The strike would last 111 days. It would be marked by bitterness, violence, and even murder, prodding some to urge the invocation of the Taft-Hartley Act as Truman had done in the days of John L. Lewis. Eventually it would become the longest coal strike in the nation's history.

The central issues of the strike focused on questions of labor stability and productivity. Both sides debated questions of the elimination of wildcat strikes and forced higher goals of productivity. At the bottom, both were non-economic issues. Alderson had been saying that neither labor stability nor productivity could ever be achieved at a bargaining table. These goals were by-products of deeper questions of dignity.

On December 12, a fortnight before Christmas Eve, Wayne received a telephone call from the minister who had threatened to expel his striking son from his home. His voice was different now, expressing entreaty rather than threats. He was asking for help. His parish was in Waynesburg, in Greene County, on the southwestern tip of Pennsylvania. He asked Wayne to come to the area as a peacemaker.

Wayne agreed, and a public meeting was scheduled for December 19, involving representatives from labor and management, community officials, and members of the news media. Wayne addressed the group and focused his remarks on the Christmas theme of "Peace on earth, good will toward men."

He asked pointedly, "How can there be peace on earth when there is no peace in the coal fields? Our Secretary of State visits Israel pursuing world peace. Why doesn't the Secretary of Labor go to the coal fields for labor peace? The President invites Begin and Sadat to Camp David to mediate their disputes. Why aren't the leaders of the BCOA and the UMW at Camp David? Where are the politicians who stood at your gates shaking hands during the election? Where are the peacemakers?"

Wayne knew that everybody wanted peace, but the basis of that peace had to be genuine. If the roots of anger and discontent were not dealt with, any peace achieved would be a flimsy peace, a guarded truce in disguise. Such truces would always be disturbed by the sounds of rattling swords. They would always be tenuous, cold wars ready to erupt into hot wars with the slightest provocation. But such "truces" were all that could be offered by the politics of confrontation.

Wayne called for a day of prayer to be climaxed by a community rally for peace. The rally was designed to be a symbolic act, which would bring people together under the umbrella of prayer to highlight the urgent need for a lasting peace. The press picked up the "peace and good will" motif, noting that at that very moment the Secretary of State was out of the country pursuing America's interests in the international cause of human rights and dignity, while at home there was misery in the coal fields.

Violent weather forced the postponement of the rally until early February. When the day finally arrived the community responded with enthusiasm, expressing strong desire that God's way, the way of valuing people, would be taken seriously by both sides in the dispute. Toward the end of the day, a coal miner stood up and spoke.

"We support all this. These are the gut issues. We are not fighting an economic war. We want dignity. We are not animals. But, Mr. Alderson, here in Western Pennsylvania we are basically conservatives. We are not the radicals. We do want peace, without violence. We appreciate it that you've come down here, but this place isn't the real hotbed. I'll bet you don't have the guts to go down to the redneck country around Charleston, West Virginia. See what happens if you talk about the Value of the Person down there. That's where the real action is."

Wayne could feel the hair on the back of his neck bristle at the challenge. He made no reply, but sat there listening to the miner's words, merely nodding his head up and down. He understood what this meant. To be a peacemaker in the midst of furious hostility is to be a human lightning rod. To work, the lightning rod must be where the lightning is flashing and striking.

Wayne drove back home, ate a hasty dinner, and started packing his suitcases. Nancy said, "Where are you going now?"

"I'm going to Charleston, West Virginia."

"What on earth for? You just got back from Waynesburg, isn't that enough for one week?"

Wayne explained the miner's challenge saying that he couldn't deny the force of the argument. If the Value of the Person was to be any help, it had to be applied at the eye of the tornado.

Nancy was adamant. "Not this time, please. You have no official invitation to be there. You can't just walk in down there and get involved. There's no reason for this."

Nancy's words made sense, but logic took second place to Wayne's gut reaction. His inner compulsion was like a powerful magnet, drawing him back out to the point.

He got behind the wheel and made the hazardous, seven-hour drive over icy roads to Charleston. That the town itself was depressed was evident. The snow was grimy with old coal dust. The river was lined with coal barges, empty and still, giving silent witness to the strike. A mood of hopelessness hung in the air.

Wayne didn't know anybody in town. He was a stranger, and the townspeople looked at him suspiciously, as if he had come from another world. Dressed in the garb of management, he looked to them like an industrial "hired gun-slinger" or a foreign intruder, like Mark Twain's "man who corrupted Hadley-ville."

Alderson checked in at a hotel and set out quickly to explore his best bet, the local churches. He made the rounds, dropping in to talk with the pastors. The response he got was both monotonous and frustrating.

"We cannot afford to get involved."

Wayne quickly realized that he would get no help from the clergy, who were as suspicious of him as the townspeople; so he turned his attention to the press. He went to a local news office and was overjoyed to find a friendly and familiar face, that of a woman reporter he had met during coverage of an earlier wildcat strike in eastern Ohio. She had seen *Miracle of Pittron* and was a supporter. Wayne explained why he was there and she nodded in understanding. She got on the phone and started making key contacts, spreading the word that the stranger in town was "OK."

The next morning, Wayne got in his car and drove around to the small communities and mining towns that dot the area. It was like the house by house, town by town strategy he had used in the war. He visited the local mayors and other public officials, showing them the film. They made the connection between the steel foundry and the coal fields, and responded with unbridled cooperation. One West Virginia mayor liked the film so much he invited fifteen other mayors from neighboring towns to gather in his office for a showing. The mountain was coming to Mohammed.

When the mayors gathered, they were surprised that Alderson knew so much about life in the coal fields. They didn't expect that from a management man. But as Wayne related his story of Lank Alderson, the company store, and the tent on the edge of Canonsburg, they realized he could be trusted. Finally, they voiced the question that was in all of their minds. "What do you want? Why are you here?"

"I want peace, not war," answered Wayne. "I'm here because I want to help people see what the real issues are. Until the

United Mine Workers and the BCOA start solving problems where they start, peace will never come."

The mayors understood. They asked Wayne if he knew Arnold Miller, the reigning president of the United Mine Workers. Wayne shook his head.

"Miller would relate to what you're doing. He should know about it. You should meet with him."

Wayne was flattered by the suggestion, but he knew it was out of the question. Miller's picture was on the front page of the paper, which featured news stories of government negotiations about the strike. Arnold Miller was in Washington, and obviously had no time to be meeting with Wayne Alderson.

Wayne returned to his hotel. He was bone weary from his week-long sojourn in redneck country. The thought struck him, *The miner in Pennsylvania was wrong. These men down here aren't really rednecks. They are the same as miners everywhere. They have the same needs, the same worries, the same gripes. The story is the same everywhere, only the accent is different.*

Wayne called Nancy as he did every day, and related the events of the day.

"Come on home, hon," she said, "you've done enough. You've been down there a week already."

Wayne refused stubbornly, arguing for more time as more work was still to be done.

"Why?" Nancy asked. "What else can you do?"

Wayne answered, almost meekly, "I don't know for certain, I just know I have to stay here a little longer. Please trust me, I'll be home Monday for sure."

The next day the phone rang in Wayne's room. When he picked up the receiver he heard a gruff voice say, "Are you the guy showing that film to people?"

Wayne admitted that he was.

"Arnold Miller wants to meet you. Will you do it?"

Wayne's voice stuck momentarily in his throat. he couldn't believe it. With effort, he replied, "Yes."

"I'll call back," the voice said, and the line went dead.

Wayne stood there staring at the receiver he was still holding in his hand, as if that piece of plastic could answer the questions that were racing through his head. *How could it be from Miller? He's in Washington. He doesn't even know me."*

Wayne's instincts made him wary. It smelled like an ambush. He waited in his room for further word, but nothing happened. He wracked his brain trying to figure out how Arnold Miller could have heard he was there. Did the mayors tell him? The newspaper reporter?

Then Wayne recalled something that had happened just a few days before he left for Charleston. He remembered an incident that evolved out of a radio talk show he and Sam Piccolo had been doing in Brownsville, Pennsylvania. The interview centered on the theme of the Value of the Person, and lasted for two hours as Wayne and Sam fielded questions from telephone callers. The call letters of the station were, ironically, WASP. It was known in the area as the "coal miners' station."

When the show was over and Wayne and Sam left the radio booth, they were greeted by a small group of miners who had been listening to the interview on a car radio. They turned the car around and drove straight to the station, waiting for Wayne and Sam to finish the broadcast.

"We've been listening to the show," said one of the men. "It's obvious to us that you understand the problems of the coal fields. We want to know if we can help. We want to find ways to implement the Value of the Person in the coal fields."

The man speaking was Rudy Medved, the current president of the Miners for Unity, an established and well respected organization within the UMW. Their objective was to create an atmosphere of trust and cooperation within the union, fearing that internal strife and splinter groups might ultimately destroy the United Mine Workers.

Back in his hotel room, Wayne wondered if it was Rudy who had alerted Miller to his activities. Surely Medved had the clout, if anyone did, to pull off such a meeting. But at this point the whole question was idle speculation, something for Wayne to think about as he waited by the silent phone.

When the silence continued into the evening, Wayne began to feel more and more foolish. Convinced that the whole thing was a hoax, he decided to go to bed. He guessed somebody was just having fun, playing cruel games with him. Wayne should have expected it, knowing full well that outsiders were not particularly welcome here. Only the day before, just across the river in Kentucky, two CBS cameramen were attacked while on location investigating the murder of a picketing miner. The men were beaten up, their camera equipment was smashed, and they were run out of town. *Maybe,* thought Wayne as he tried to turn his mind off to sleep, *my turn will be next.*

The next morning Alderson was jolted from sleep by the jangling phone. He rolled over and sleepily groped for the phone, thinking it was the hotel wake-up call. He heard the gruff voice again.

"Miller wants to meet you tomorrow morning at 10 A.M. He'll be in the private dining room of the Sheraton Inn. Will you be there?"

Again Wayne answered "yes," and the man abruptly hung up. Now all Alderson could do was wait it out to see if the meeting was authentic. Wayne got dressed leisurely, and went downstairs to eat breakfast and pass the time relaxing in the lobby of the Charleston House. In the lobby he spotted another familiar face. It was Lil Swanson, a veteran correspondent for United Press International. The two exchanged pleasantries, and settled down to discuss the strike. Wayne answered Lil's questions concerning his presence there, and then casually mentioned that he was waiting around to meet with Arnold Miller.

Lil was amused.

"No way, friend. Somebody's playing games and you're it. Right now everybody in the country wants to talk to Arnold Miller. Haven't you heard? The negotiations have broken off and Miller is in seclusion somewhere. No one can even find him. Why would he want to see you? Sorry, pal, you've been had."

Wayne felt the now familiar feelings of foolishness welling up inside. He didn't know how to answer her questions. They were all the same questions he'd been asking himself. Like a little boy who boasts when he's been challenged, Wayne said in less than convincing tones, "Well, come along with me and see for yourself."

Lil was flabbergasted. She agreed to go along. She still didn't believe Wayne, but she didn't want to miss out on a possible scoop.

Lil and Wayne rendezvoused the next morning and made their way to the Sheraton. They went to the private dining room, both feeling edgy and apprehensive. The door was standing open. He looked inside and there was Arnold Miller, flanked by two of his "special assistants," obviously bodyguards.

Miller rose to shake hands and make introductions. Wayne introduced Lil and asked permission for her to sit in on the meeting. Miller said, "Let her stay."

Miller started the conversation by telling Wayne he had heard all about his recent activities, indicating the reports had been favorable. He spoke abruptly, from the shoulder.

"Alderson, I have two questions I want to ask you. First, why in the hell do you care what happens to the miners when no one else does? Second, who's paying you to be here?"

Wayne answered the questions one at a time. To the first, he responded by relating his family background and his vision for the Value of the Person. He explained that he was there in no official capacity. He was not a negotiator, nor a federal mediator, but simply a deeply concerned Christian and son of a coal miner. Then Wayne squared off to give answer to the second question.

"Who's paying me? Let me answer that straight and clear. No one. I'm on nobody's payroll. I'm here strictly on my own. This trip is coming out of my pocket, nobody else's."

The men spent two hours in conversation, quickly developing a rapport. Wayne found Miller to be compassionate. He carried an obvious burden of concern for his miners and their families. In the discussion the men discovered they had much in common. Wayne noticed that part of Miller's ear was missing. He asked directly, "What happened to your ear?"

Miller shot back, "What happened to your head? How'd you get a hole in it?"

They both laughed and started exchanging war stories. Arnold Miller had been shot at Omaha Beach during the Normandy Invasion. The bullet entered his mouth and came out the side of his head, clipping off a piece of his ear in the process.

The conversation came to an end with Miller praising the Value of the Person concept. He said, "This concept should be a top priority matter for both labor and management when the strike ends. We will need something like this to heal the wounds and the unresolved issues."

Wayne startled Miller by asking if he would like them to pray together. Miller looked at Wayne and said, "No one's ever asked me that before."

Right there the men bowed their heads and prayed together, as Lil and the bodyguards looked on in disbelief. Lil had been taking copious notes of the conversation. Now she couldn't resist snapping a picture of Wayne Alderson and Arnold Miller praying together. She had her scoop, and the story and her picture were on the UPI wires that afternoon.

As Wayne rose to leave, Miller reached out gently to stop him. "Wait a minute, Wayne. I have a luncheon date with Jay Rockefeller. Why don't you come along and we can talk some more?"

Wayne went with Miller to visit Governor Rockefeller. Miller told the Governor about Wayne's work, and Rockefeller was intrigued. The agenda was forgotten as the men became absorbed in conversation about the relevance of the Value of the Person concept to the coal strike. Later that afternoon, Governor Rockefeller's Press Secretary issued a proclamation endorsing the Value of the Person concept for the coal fields, and supporting a National Day of Prayer.

Arnold Miller drove Wayne back to his hotel and the two men shook hands and parted. Wayne hurriedly packed his bags, checked out of the Charleston House, and drove back to Pitts-

Arnold Miller, President of the United Mine Workers Union, and Wayne share a moment of prayer in Charleston, West Virginia, during the bitter 110-day coal strike. January 1978.

burgh. He could hardly wait to tell Nancy what had transpired that day.

Wayne was gaining a reputation not only as a labor-management consultant, but also as a peacemaker. He remembered the words of Jesus, "Blessed are the peacemakers, for they shall be called the sons of God." Wayne wanted to be known as a child of God.

He knew there were all kinds of "peacemakers" in the world. There was the type that wanted peace at any price, a peace with no honor, based not on reconciliation but on selling out one side or the other. He remembered the famous news photo of Neville Chamberlain leaning over his balcony in London, holding his umbrella. Chamberlain had just returned from Munich and was announcing to England, "There has come to Downing Street peace with honor . . . peace in our time." At that very moment, Adolf Hitler was mobilizing his army for the Blitzkrieg.

Then there was the type of peacemaker who tells both sides exactly what they want to hear. He is for whomever he is with at the moment. Such peacemakers only serve to increase hostility while they fill their pockets with fees.

Wayne's model of the ideal peacemaker is Jesus, the Prince of Peace. The true peacemaker cares about both sides. He speaks the truth as he sees it, becoming a human lightning rod if he has to, absorbing the hostility of both parties as he stands in the middle. To Wayne, that's what the cross symbolized. In death, Jesus bore the wrath of God at the hands of furious men in an act of cosmic reconciliation. If Wayne was going to follow Jesus, he had to expect flak from both sides of the labor-management trenches. His expectations would be realized soon enough.

The coal strike continued to drag on, and the dwindling coal supply was becoming a major threat to American industry. The winter was almost past and March began with a hint of spring in the air. On Sunday, March 5, Wayne led a major prayer rally in the middle of Market Square in downtown Pittsburgh. This rally attracted nationwide attention. Not only were Pittsburgh's media giving full coverage, but the Christian Broadcast Network filmed the entire event for national coverage. CBN ran a full fifteen-minute segment of it across the nation, including broadcasts in Hawaii.

Hundreds of people crowded the square to hear the scheduled speakers, among them Wayne, Reid Carpenter, president of the Pittsburgh Leadership Foundation; John Guest, rector of

St. Stephen's Episcopal Church; Lefty Scumaci, and Tom Skinner, leader of the Black Christian Evangelical Association and Chaplain of the Washington Redskins. At the last minute, another speaker was enlisted.

Just before the meeting began, a coal miner from the Pittsburgh area approached Wayne belligerently, pouring out hatred. It was bitterly cold for March, and the young man was dressed in a flimsy jacket that was faded and torn. Moving his feet and rubbing his arms in a futile effort to warm himself, he handed Wayne a piece of paper with a poem written on it, insisting that he be allowed to read it at the rally. Wayne read the poem to himself. What it lacked in artistic grace it made up for with powerful, emotional words of anger. It was full of venemous hatred, referring to management personnel as "cold-blooded murderers." Wayne lifted his eyes from the paper and spoke softly, "I can't let you read that. We're here for a prayer rally, not to add fuel to the fire. We're here to promote love and peace, not more hatred and war."

Wayne's words stung the miner, and it registered on his face. "I'm not going to call on you to read your poem," Wayne continued, "but I am going to call on you to pray for management."

The man's lips curled in a sardonic smile, and what color was left vanished from his face. Alderson must be joking. But Wayne's eyes didn't blink as he stared expectantly at the miner, waiting for a response. The defiant grin slowly vanished, and he shuffled his feet in uncertainty.

"But I've never prayed out loud in front of people. I don't know how to pray. What will I say?"

Wayne's piercing gaze warmed into a smile.

"Don't worry about it, God will give you the words."

During the rally, Wayne looked over at him. The miner feebly nodded his head indicating that he was ready. Wayne called him forward to pray, taking a silent gulp of air as he played out his gamble. Speaking into the microphone haltingly, obviously straining for control, the miner's prayer was the poetry of the people.

Nancy Alderson was standing at the rear of the square behind the crowd of people. The words of the leaders came clearly over the loudspeakers, but she didn't hear them. Her attention was riveted on a car that kept driving slowly around the square. It was a large black Cadillac limousine, the kind one might expect to see parked imperiously in front of the Waldorf Astoria, or along Broadway on opening night. But there was no neatly attired chauffeur or silver-haired executive behind the wheel. The men in the car looked like gorillas; they were hard looking, wearing the uniform of the underworld. They never stopped the car to get out. They merely kept watching the area, listening intently as if on a mission of surveillance. When the rally ended, the car disappeared.

Nancy was shuddering from the experience. She told Wayne about it and asked him who they were. Wayne had noticed them too. He had no idea who they were or whom they represented, but he was sure they weren't mafia. He filed it in the back of his mind and calmly told Nancy not to worry about it. But Nancy's fears were not so easily assuaged. Maybe Wayne could take it in soldier's stride, but not Nancy. Wayne never discovered who the men in the car were—they could have represented any number of concerns hostile to the Value of the Person Movement.

Five days later, the coal strike was settled and the nation breathed a collective sigh of relief. After sixteen weeks of paralysis, the miners went back to the pits and the coal barges were moving down the Ohio River again. A new contract was signed, but a time of healing was urgently required—the strike had left open wounds and deep scars in its wake.

As the coal strike was in its final hours, Wayne was deluged with paper work, correspondence, and requests for speaking and training seminars. It was more than he could handle alone, and he needed help badly. Nancy urged him to hire someone full time to be his assistant and to coordinate the seminars.

At the same time, Wayne's daughter Nancy Jean was finishing the final months of her senior year at Grove City College and searching the job market in earnest. She was conscious of the rapid changes that were taking place in the work world, and the new doors that were opening up for women. She was part of the new generation of women who were preparing to assume a full role in business, letting competence rule over prejudice.

Already tapped for *Who's Who in American Colleges and Universities,* Nancy Jean was looking beyond graduation, which would include the notation on the program, magna cum laude. Her double major in Communication Arts and Education equipped her for a variety of career opportunities. Her background in summer employment at Pittron and her exposure to the inside machinations of the corporate world gave her a head start over other graduates. Her poise was notable as she went through the senior syndrome of job applications and interviews. She didn't suffer from a case of academic cynicism, but she was not dazzled by the promises made by campus recruiters for large corporations. She was aware of the fact that all was not well in the inner sanctum of the home office or the boardroom.

"I was wary, perhaps a bit jaundiced by all the strife I was exposed to, by seeing Dad walking into the middle of labor disputes, and from listening to the men from the foundry talk about the turmoil of their lives. As I went through the interviews and the escorted tours through business facilities, I had a sense that the guides weren't showing me all that was there. The recruiters don't usually talk about the frustration, backbiting, and pain that I knew was there not so deeply buried behind the scene. With each conducted tour my mind was provoked by the urgent need for the Value of the Person. I knew that behind the scenes there were people crying out for visible and tangible proof of love, dignity, and respect. These thoughts and memories kept surfacing as graduation approached, but I kept pushing them back. Frankly, I didn't want to get involved with it. I saw the grief which Dad didn't let many people see. I wanted to be part of a stable company, an established organization which would offer the kind of security I had before Dad got fired."

Despite the fact that Nancy Jean was graduating at a time when the job market was at low ebb, she received two attractive job offers. Both afforded her the opportunity to develop her skills and implement her training, both offered the level of financial security she desired. Her choice in the matter was not between good and bad options, but the much more difficult decision between rival goods. As she halted between the two alternatives, she began to feel an inner restlessness about her future. Rationally, she could see nothing wrong with either of the job offers—both were for legitimate work, both were in line with her gifts, talents, and educational preparation. But inside, feelings were starting to churn that robbed her of peace within.

In the meantime, Wayne was searching for an assistant. He dutifully read resumes and interviewed candidates, looking for someone he could depend upon to understand the real heartbeat of the work.

Nancy Jean was aware of her father's quest for help. She also knew she could make no final decision about the starting phase of her career without first going to the mat and wrestling it out fervently in prayer.

"I knew prayer had to be a real part of my decision-making process," she recalled. "After all, that's what it's all about. I had to be sure that, whatever job I chose, I would have the opportunity to glorify God in the bottom line. The deadline for my decision was on me, and I still didn't know which job to take. So I just got forceful with God about it. I went alone to the college chapel and entered into marathon negotiations with God."

Two days later, her negotiations with God still deadlocked, Nancy Jean received an invitation from a church in Grove City to come and show the film *Miracle of Pittron* and to address the congregation on the Value of the Person concept. This was the first time anyone had ever asked her—instead of her father—

to do the job. The very next day she received a call to do the same thing in Butler, Pennsylvania.

"I guess maybe I was secretly hoping that God would give me some sign from heaven. Instead, it came from earth. It suddenly all made sense. I realized my indecision about the jobs was rooted in the fact that I had the Value of the Person in my heart. I knew then that's where I had to be at this time in my life, at least temporarily, until Dad had a chance to get things consolidated. So I called Dad and applied for the position he was trying to fill."

Wayne's response to his daughter's "application" was characteristically Alderson. "Why not?" was his answer. Of course, Wayne was moved by Nancy Jean's decision to join him on the point. Though he shared the protective sense of most fathers toward their offspring, he also shared that enormous sense of pride that flows when a son or daughter elects to follow in one's footsteps. Setting fears of charges of nepotism aside, Wayne warmly embraced Nancy Jean as his partner in ministry.

In some respects, Nancy Jean is a carbon copy of her mother. She has the same fair skin and blonde hair, and she dresses with the same taste and style. Her mother's "Betty Grable" legs peek out of Nancy Jean's narrow skirts. Bright blue eyes mirror the many facets of her personality, now revealing charming warmth, then a seriousness. Those same blue eyes can flash with storm warnings for those who underestimate her or seek to patronize her womanhood. Nancy Jean combines the gentility of her mother with an urbanity that communicates competence.

As director of the Value of the Person seminars, Nancy Jean carries out her responsibilities with professionalism. She is comfortable dealing with coal miners or board chairmen, union officials or reporters. She is the "detail person," making sure nothing slips through the cracks in organizing the work of seminars or major conclaves like the International Labor-Management Prayer Breakfast. Her communication skills are apparent when she speaks to large groups, and she is the first person exposed to the heat of audiences—which usually means dealing with hostility and cynicism. She goes first because her engaging style is best suited for disarming the skeptics. On the seminar tour, Wayne is often relegated to the position of second scout as Nancy Jean stands on the point of the program.

Perhaps her most valuable asset to Wayne and his male associates is her ability to read people. Sitting in on lengthy discussions with labor leaders or business executives, Nancy Jean has the ability to listen between the lines. When such meetings are over and it is post-mortem time, Lefty or Wayne will turn to her and say, "What do you think?"

Nancy then gives her impressions of the meeting, noting the subtleties of body language. She can pick out the hustlers and insincere with unusual accuracy, quickly spotting the flim-flam types. The men have come to rely on Nancy's sixth sense and often place more trust in her evaluations than they do in their own.

One of Nancy Jean's first tasks was to help Wayne respond to a request that came from Dr. Jack Troyanovich, the newly appointed director of training of the Volkswagen auto assembly plant in New Stanton, Pennsylvania. Troyanovich, who had spent seventeen years as a university professor, inquired about Wayne's availability and interest in being involved in preliminary training seminars for the new plant.

Volkswagen had recently located their assembly operation in a huge complex that had been constructed by Chrysler and abandoned at the last minute. Three states had been competing vigorously for Volkswagen's presence. It would be the first foreign auto assembly plant to be located in the United States, a rare political plumb. The governors of the three states wooing VW were countering each other's bids with enticing offers. The suspense lasted for several months before Volkswagen made its final decision. Governor Milton Shapp finally prevailed, and VW came to Pennsylvania. There was jubilation in the western part of the state at the announcement. A modern industrial giant was coming to town, giving Pittsburgh's sagging economy and rising unemployment rate much needed relief.

Troyanovich met Wayne at New Stanton, where they were joined by Ira Fine, Labor Editor of the *Pittsburgh Press.* Troyanovich told them how he had stumbled upon the Value of the Person Program.

His wife, Carol, had been wrapping the garbage in newspaper when her eye caught the fragments of a headline partially buried beneath coffee grounds, vegetable peels, meat scraps, and the like: *WORKER VALUE FOR LABOR PEACE.* The dateline was Labor Day, 1977. She dumped the garbage onto a fresh piece of paper, trying to decipher the story that was partly obliterated by garbage stains. It was an article about Alderson and the Value of the Person, written by Ira Fine. Carol Troyanovich showed the greasy paper to her husband. He liked what he read and took it from there, thinking, *This is exactly what VW needs.* Troyanovich secured permission from Richard Cummins, the plant manager, to approach Wayne about participating in an experimental training seminar. The men met together in Cummins' office, where the plant manager endorsed the experiment with one half-serious proviso: "I can't have a goddamned chapel built in here."

Alderson met Cummins' joke head on. "I'm not about building chapels. It is not my objective to put chapels in factories or to turn the workplace into a church. The whole world is talking about the new car you're making here, the Rabbit. My goal here is that the Value of the Person should be greater than the Value of the Rabbit. I won't be used to manipulate a work force. I will not be an industrial prostitute. I will walk away the minute I'm persuaded that you're not fully committed to implementing the program."

Cummins, a straightforward leader, was a veteran of the Detroit labor wars. He was familiar with Alderson's style, and agreed with Wayne's terms.

Cummins took Wayne and Ira for a tour of the plant. Only a skeleton crew was working, giving the finishing touches to the lines and gearing things up for production. The inside of the plant was a stark contrast from what Wayne had been accustomed to at Pittron. The place was immaculate, gleaming with fresh paint and shiny new machinery. It was a completely modern facility, almost antiseptic. The physical environment was much more conducive to worker morale than anything Pittron had seen in its finest hour.

The training plan was outlined. Volkswagen was going to select fifty-six persons from its initial work force of about two hundred rank and file. These fifty-six were to go through a thirty-day period of concentrated training to become first line supervisors. Three of those days would be given over to training on the Value of the Person, to be held at the Ligonier Valley Study Center, a few miles down the Pennsylvania Turnpike from New Stanton. Troyanovich coordinated the training plans, which featured seminars by Alderson, Piccolo, Scumaci, and others.

The fifty-six persons selected came to the Center in March. They were new to Volkswagen, but veterans of the labor arena. For the most part they were skeptical of training that had any religious overtones to it. Though many sat through the seminars with arms and legs crossed defensively, there were signs of hope in their eyes. They wanted things to be different, and hoped that they could duplicate at VW the miracle of Pittron, but at the same time they were afraid to believe it.

At the end of the three days, however, they were more enthusiastic. At the end of the seminar, the candidates for supervisor were given an opportunity to express themselves. Their responses were emotionally laden with determination to implement the concept.

One of the fifty-six, Jim Swope, had been one of the first men hired at VW and was part of the original team of United Auto Workers at the plant. Swope was about to leave labor and join the ranks of management via a promotion to first line supervisor. He was so moved by the Value of the Person Seminar that he made a critical decision about his own career. He decided that day to decline the promotion and to stay with the union rank and file in order to work for the implementation of the Value of the Person.

This was to be the extent of the Volkswagen seminars. However, the first class of fifty-six were so inspired by its experience that they drew up a petition asking Cummins to have the whole work force trained in the program. The petition was signed by fifty-five of the group. The lone dissenter expressed admiration for the program but was convinced that management would never allow it and that to sign the petition would be useless.

The text of the petition read:

Dear Mr. Cummins,

We can't express in words the gratitude and appreciation we feel to yourself and Volkswagen in attending the first supervisory class. The impact these last thirty days had left on us will not be forgotten on our jobs at Volkswagen and the future in our lives.

In writing this letter, we would like to point out one important and valuable tool that we will be using continuously in all aspects of our work and in our daily lives. In this Mr. Cummins, is the Value of the Person.

After coming together for the last time on March 31 with all the people at the Ligonier Valley Study Center, we know we are in the right direction as a Volkswagen family. Now that we are to return to our regular jobs, the one person that sticks out in our minds because of what he had done to enlighten this concept in us is Mr. Wayne Alderson. We would like Volkswagen Manufacturing of America to give close consideration of continuing this concept in the plant here at New Stanton, through the direction of Mr. Alderson. We think as a group that it would not only be a major asset to the person, but also to the company as a whole.

We recommend that this program become one of the basic programs for new hourly workers, present hourly workers, and *all* levels of management. We contend that any individual involved in the plant that does not have the opportunity to attend the program will be without an important tool needed to achieve our goals.

Thanks again and may you be blessed in your efforts.

Cummins read the petition and considered the request, waiting for input from Detroit. In the meantime, the press was having a field day. The training sessions received widespread publicity, perhaps too much. Most of it was positive and encouraging, some of it cynical. One local newspaper headlined the event with, *IT'S STRICTLY CARROT, NOT STICK, AT RABBIT PLANT* Another read, *VW: LITTLE BIT OF HEAVEN.*

Positive statements appeared on the front page of the *Wall Street Journal* and in the news section of *Industry Week.* The nation was watching Volkswagen to see if it would, indeed, become a model. As time dragged on and the decision was delayed, many of the original fifty-six trainees grew disheartened.

Finally, the word came back from VW. Alderson was asked to lead a training seminar for Cummins' management team and for the two thousand hourly workers who were being hired. One crucial group was omitted from the training against Alderson's wishes; the newly elected officers of the UAW.

Volkswagen had high goals. Its target was the production of two hundred thousand Rabbits a year. To reach that goal they could not afford strikes, absenteeism, or industrial sabotage. They shared the growing concern of the auto industry about the multiplication of annual recalls of cars discovered with dangerously defective parts. Such recalls were not always caused by poor engineering design or mechanical deficiencies; they were often the direct result of worker sabotage, which expressed a desire for revenge against the company. Everybody knew that.

Cummins' management team verbally embraced the training program and talked about implementing it in the plant. In the meantime, Wayne and Nancy Jean began training the new hourly workers who were being hired. During the weeks of training, Wayne started getting feedback from inside the plant that the program was not being implemented. He asked for permission to go into the plant, but it was denied. That was a red flag.

Wayne phoned Cummins and spoke candidly about the discouraging rumors he was hearing, reminding him of the agreement they had made to make the implementation of the Value of the Person a top management priority. Alderson said, "Dick, I will do no more training until your management team starts to implement the program. I meant what I said about that—I will not be used to manipulate a work force."

With those words, Alderson terminated his contract with VW, leaving the ball in management's court. He followed up the phone call with a letter dated September 11, 1978.

As you know, in August we completed the first phase of the Value of the Person training seminars. . . . Everyone involved in these seminars, including you and your staff, agreed that this phase was most successful and was an encouragement to all, for it demonstrated that we were on the right track to making Volkswagen a model plant.

However, Phase Two of the program is long overdue and its implementation must now become a top priority. A conscious and committed step must be taken in order to make the successful transition from "Outside Training" to "Inside Implementation" where the Value of the Person is expressed by example from within the organization. As discussed throughout our training, the Value of the Person within Volkswagen will not become a reality by mere training, but rather by the boldness of its people in implementing the teachings through personal example.

The rumblings at VW were heralded by a news article that appeared in the Greensburg *Tribune-Review* under the heading, *LABOR/MANAGEMENT ACCORD SKIDS AT VW*. The press, alienated by Volkswagen's public relations policies toward the media, trained a broadside attack on VW's management failure to implement the Value of the Person, frustrating the workers and moving them toward dangerous levels of disillusionment.

A few weeks after Alderson left, the New Stanton plant experienced its first work stoppage in the form of a wildcat strike. VW didn't have a chapel built, but it didn't have the Value of the Person either. Cummins contacted Wayne.

"I think we've been too slow in implementing the program,"

he admitted. "Maybe this strike will benefit all of us. When the men come back, I'll do all I can to implement it."

The strike did not produce the hoped for benefits. Perhaps a key to the sequence of events may be found in Cummins' words, "I'll do all I can. . . ." Within three months Cummins was gone, resigning to take a position elsewhere. His resignation added fuel to the speculation that his efforts to implement the Value of the Person were being torpedoed by Detroit and by some members of his own staff. Reports of deteriorating conditions continued to leak from the plant, along with insinuations that management was caught up in an internal power struggle which diverted its attention from the work force.

More work stoppages occurred, but VW never called Alderson to return, although he had left them with a standing offer to return if needed. As Wayne traversed the country he grew weary at hearing the same question over and over again, "What happened at Volkswagen?" Since Cummins had left and Alderson had no access to the plant, it was difficult to know for sure what ultimately happened there. But the labor unrest is a well-documented fact at the New Stanton plant.

Alderson learned a painful lesson from the Volkswagen experiment: if the Value of the Person concept is to work, it must be fully backed by management. Alderson continues to do labor-management seminars and training sessions, but only on the condition that top management makes a firm commitment to implementation.

Alderson still retains hope for the future of Volkswagen, New Stanton. Many of those trained in the Value of the Person are working inside the plant to see the program materialize. In August of 1979, Wayne was contacted by Jim Swope. Swope informed Alderson that Local 2055 of the UAW was sponsoring its first Labor Day rally for the employees of VW and their families. Congressman John Dent and Ray Ross, regional director (2A) of the UAW, were slated to address the rally. Swope asked Wayne if he could come and address the crowd.

On Labor Day Wayne, a management man, rose to give the

keynote address at a labor rally. He could see hundreds of Value of the Person pins being worn by the rank and file in the audience in front of him. Wayne gave a challenge to the workers assembled there:

"The Volkswagen plant stands at a crossroads—you can choose to go man's way of confrontation or God's way of reconciliation. You can choose to become another jungle or you can become a model plant for the world to see. You cannot escape the choice. No choice *is* a choice. No choice is to accept things as they are—and they are unacceptable. My prayer is that Volkswagen will be known not as the place that rejected the Value of the Person, but as the auto assembly plant that pioneered it."

Wayne went home from the rally carrying a blue hat and a tee-shirt that symbolized his warm reception and honorary membership in Local 2055 of the UAW.

No great leader has an umblemished success record. Washington had his Brandywine, MacArthur his Bataan. Wayne Alderson met his most frustrating setback at Volkswagen in New Stanton, Pennsylvania.

The measure of a man must be found in how he handles his disappointments as well as his triumphs. Disappointment can easily be the catalyst to personal defeatism, for trying not quite so hard the next time, for opting for safer routes of progress— or it can ignite the reserves of one's deepest levels of determination. Wayne Alderson's aversion to defeat is almost pathological. He has contempt for those who compromise quickly, or retreat at the first sign of a casualty. He knows that no worthy victory is without casualties. He knew it in Germany and he knows it now. Volkswagen was a high-casualty mission for him. It haunts him to this day.

# 9

# Work-World
# Reformation: First
# Call to Breakfast

After Volkswagen, Alderson was left with a confusing
set of circumstances. On the one hand, the national exposure
from the Volkswagen training session was bringing numerous
inquiries from other companies seeking new methods to bring
labor peace to their operations. The publicity brought both
fame and credibility, and Alderson's voice was beginning to be
heard in high places. Yet, at the same time, the rumblings of
discontent from VW's rank and file gave the critics ammunition
with which to shoot him down. The experiment that had cata-
pulted him to the pages of *Industry Week* and the *Wall Street
Journal* was now getting a measure of bad press.

Again Wayne felt the pressure of being on the point. The
press attention was like a spotlight picking him out in the midst
of a night patrol. His every move could be seen plainly by friend
and enemy alike. The early days of obscurity were gone, and
along with them the luxury of the surprise attack. His first

response was to run for cover—to escape from the blinding light. But that would be to embrace the methods of darkness.

To retreat now would be to surrender to the enemy and quench the hopes of those left in the trenches behind him. Alderson still thinks in terms of war. Though committed to peace, he realizes the irony of having to fight to achieve it.

Alderson had stirred up hostility against himself that was concentrated in one special segment of the work world—the professional arbitrators and labor attorneys. One would think that such professional peacemakers would welcome him as a comrade. Not so—to them he was a threat, a maverick who endangered the traditional methods of negotiation and reconciliation.

The American Association of Arbitrators invited Wayne to address their annual convention in upstate New York. Wayne was being asked to come into the den of his chief critics. The meeting would be comprised of professional negotiators and federal mediators, men and women paid for their services of "reconciliation," yet who profited by continued confrontation. Without agitation and confrontation, these people would have no reason to exist; they would be without jobs. Thus they had a vested interest in continued labor-management conflict. Wayne regarded them as the "money changers" of the industrial temple.

Lefty warned Wayne not to attend the convention. "Don't go," he said, "they'll eat you alive."

But Alderson went . . . alone. The program began with the showing of *Miracle of Pittron.* As Wayne sat through the film, he was aware of the hostility in the room. He was hoping the portrayal of the men of Pittron might soften his adversaries, but it wasn't working. As soon as the lights were switched on again, the negative reaction was swift. Their target was the religious aspect of the film.

"What are you trying to pull? You're just peddling religion! What about the Jews? What about the people who don't buy into all the Christian stuff? This is no place for preaching!"

The questions, sounding more like accusations than inquiries, came in a volley. Before Wayne could answer one, another was shouted at him.

Finally, Wayne got mad.

"Hold it!" he said. "You don't know what the hell you're talking about. Yes—I'm a Christian. That's what motivates me. I never apologize for that or compromise it. Without that, frankly, I wouldn't give a damn about all this, about any of you. But I'm not here to peddle Christianity—I'm pushing the Value of the Person. That's what my Christianity commits me to. But you don't have to be a Christian to value people. The very thing you hate and fight against—prejudice—is what you are spitting out right now. You're prejudging me and condemning me for what I believe. Look at the hostility in this room. Who's going to mediate that? Who's going to reconcile us?"

The debate, interspersed with heated arguments and rising voices lasted four hours. Finally, one of the most respected of the Jewish leaders rose to speak.

"I've been sitting here listening to all this. I want to say that in my opinion, you are a man of God. Don't stop what you are doing; you're not a threat to me or my Jewishness. You're simply a threat to human greed."

The next day Alderson challenged the group, hitting hard. "I am for arbitration and mediation, but my goal is to make your jobs unnecessary, to eliminate the growth of your business. I would like to see you plan a conference on planning your own elimination. Right now you are the only winners, you're laughing all the way to the bank. You are living testimony to the failure of labor and management to resolve their differences."

The challenge was greeted by spontaneous applause. When it subsided, however, a black man who was obviously not numbered with the applauders rose to speak. He demanded that Wayne give more precise explanations for his program.

"What do you mean by love, dignity, and respect?"

Wayne stared at him for a moment and finally responded, "Do I have to explain these things to *you?* You should get up here and explain them to everyone here. You should be an expert on these matters. You know very well when you *don't* have them."

The meeting ended in peace. Many of the people there avowed their support for the Value of the Person. Those who remained in opposition left with at least a measure of respect for Wayne. He was obviously not of the "soft" mold that so many of them had imagined Christian leaders to be.

Alderson's return to Pittsburgh was marked by sorrowful tidings. He was notified that his mother, Edith, was dead, stricken with a fatal heart attack in the middle of the night. There was no last vigil, no opportunity for final farewells. The matriarch of the Alderson family, the woman who kept the children together in a tent, was gone.

Wayne's father Lank had died in 1946 of heart failure. Edith waited to remarry until all her children were married, the last being Wayne in 1953. Two years later Edith married "Big John" Jacanin, who was later forced into early retirement by the effects of black lung disease. It was Big John who bore the sad tidings of Edith's death, and who stood by Wayne's side in front of his mother's casket. Wayne's mind drifted back to a conversation he had had with his mother on Easter Sunday of 1977.

Edith went into the hospital during Holy Week. She was scheduled for exploratory surgery, and her doctors suspected she was suffering from cancer. She was nervous and apprehensive, fearing the results of the probe. Nancy and Nancy Jean had visited her earlier, leaving her a Bible as a gift. Edith had grown up in the church and sung in the choir as a young girl, but she drifted away from it in her adult years. Clutching the Bible in her gnarled hands, she asked her son about his faith.

"What's all this business about being a 'Christian' you're always talking about?"

Wayne awkwardly flipped the pages of the Bible open to St. John's Gospel, finding it difficult to "instruct" his mother in such

matters. He read to her of faith and love. Edith listened intently
and finally spoke, with tears in her eyes.

"I don't have any problem with love. I love you and all the
kids."

Wayne's voice cracked with emotion as he uttered painful
words. "Mother . . . that's the first time you ever said you loved
me. In all these years I've never heard you say that. You never
said you loved me or any of the kids."

"I know, Wayne," she replied in grave tones, "I couldn't.
Can't you understand that? I couldn't afford to show love—it
would have been a weakness. It's a hard world, I had to make
you tough, all of you . . . otherwise I knew you'd never make
it. I never heard you crying or feeling sorry for yourself when
you got fired. That's how I loved you, I made you tough. Do you
realize what it took to keep you all together in the tent? I didn't
say it with words, I showed you. It's the same with God. I want
to know God like you do, but I don't know how."

The difficult dialogue continued, and finally Wayne and his
mother held hands and prayed out loud together for the first
time in their lives. Edith faced her surgery with peace, and was
relieved by the verdict that no malignancy was discovered.

Wayne pondered these memories as he walked away from his
mother's coffin. At the cemetery, the last words spoken over the
dead took on special meaning for him. "Ashes to ashes dust to
dust. . . ."

*It's a fitting farewell,* thought Wayne. *Coal dust and ashes
were what she knew best. The land was always a part of her life.*

His mother's death made Wayne reflective. He thought again
of St. Avold, of Red Preston, Billy Weaver, and Joe Stankowski.
All these people dear to him were dead, but he was still alive,
driven with a sense of mission yet unfulfilled. The rudeness of
death made him ask again, *Where is God in all this?*

Lefty and Wayne had talked many times about the role of
God in the marketplace. They knew that America had embraced secularism—a perspective that banished God from the

public sector. Perhaps God was still alive in the churches, but He was in exile from the work world. They were aware of attempts to change all that in other spheres of public life, symbolized by the prayer breakfasts that were growing in popularity in Washington, D.C., and in local satellite programs around the nation. There were the Presidential Prayer Breakfast, the Senate, Congressional, and Judicial breakfasts—all of these were designed to impress upon the public consciousness the sovereignty of God over human government. But what about the work-world? Here was where God was most needed, yet was most noticeably absent.

Lefty made the proposal. "Why not a major prayer breakfast, bringing the leadership of labor and management together under an umbrella of prayer?" This aroused Wayne's immediate interest. He was convinced that there was no neutral zone of human activity beyond the concern of God. Though not a theologian, Wayne was convinced that the nation needed to be awakened to a theology of work. Intuitively, Alderson knew the problems of labor and management were ultimately theological.

From the beginning of creation, God had identified Himself with work. The origin of work, the mandate of work, the sanctity of work, and the purpose of work are all rooted in the nature of God Himself. The Judaeo–Christian God is not a God of leisure, but of labor.

In 1942, while her native Britain was caught up in the imbroglio of World War II, with factories producing at a frantic wartime pace, author Dorothy L. Sayers contemplated the postwar future of the West. She expressed her sentiments—shared by T. S. Eliot in his poem *The Wasteland*—in an essay entitled "Why Work?"

Unless we change our whole way of thought about work, I do not think we shall ever escape from the appalling squirrel-cage of economic confusion in which we have been madly turning for the last three centuries or so; the cage in which we landed ourselves by acquiescing in a social system based on Envy and Avarice. A society in which consumption has to be artificially stimulated in order to keep production going is a society founded on trash and waste, and such a society is a house built upon sand.*

The point of labor is not to create trash.

Following the model of God's labor of creation, we see that not only the *worker,* but *work* itself has dignity. With the divine activity of labor comes also God's own benediction— "That's good." When we read the Genesis account of humanity's fall into corruption, we see that a curse is put upon human labor:

. . . cursed is the ground for thy sake;
in sorrow shalt thou eat of it all the days of thy life.
Thorns and thistles shall it bring forth to thee;
and thou shall eat the herb of the field;
In the sweat of thy face shalt thou eat bread,
till thou return unto the ground. (Gen. 3:17b–19a)

Because of thorns and sweat, it would be easy to assume that man's curse is work itself. Such a conclusion would be specious. The curse is *added* to work; work becomes more difficult because of it—but the curse is *not* work itself. The sweat of the farmer behind the plow, the miner in the pit, the steelworker in the open hearth testifies to the difficulty of labor but not the ignominy of it. The curse added because of sin never destroys the basic dignity of labor. Man—before the fall—was created for and called to work. Again, Dorothy Sayers says,

I ask that work be looked upon—not as a necessary drudgery to be undergone for the purpose of making money, but as a way of life in which the nature of man should find its proper exercise and delight and so fulfill itself to the glory of God.**

The dignity of the worker and the dignity of work are inseparably bound to each other. If the worker is demeaned, the work

*Dorothy L. Sayers, *Why Work?* (London: Methuen, 1942), p. 3.
**Ibid.

is likewise demeaned. Conversely, if we demean a person's work we demean the person.

Someone once remarked, "God doesn't make junk." In creation, God's work receives His own benediction. His work is excellent, it's quality without blemish. We who are created in the Divine image, are called not only to imitate our Creator by working—we are called to do our work well. God's labor is characterized by a quality of artistic craftsmanship. Even in redemption, the work of Christ in bringing transformation to human lives is described Biblically as "craftsmanship." Thus to do good work is a responsibility God gives to all of us. The worker on the assemblyline who vents his anger against management by acts of industrial sabotage insults God and demeans himself. To turn out sloppy work is to act against one's own personal dignity. To take pride in the excellence of one's work is not arrogance, but obedience. It is to find a deep level of human fulfillment in a job well done.

Genesis portrays humanity-in-creation as given work not as a curse but as a privilege. We are given "dominion" over the earth; the earth is to submit to our labor. Yet with that position of privilege comes responsibility. We are commanded "to dress, till, and replenish" the earth. The object of labor is not greed. The earth is to be replenished and adorned by human labor. To exploit and pollute the earth is a monstrous sin against creation; to oppress human workers evokes the wrath of God. Work was never designed to crush the human spirit. Where and when it does, it becomes a theological issue of the first magnitude.

To banish or exile God from the work world is to defy God's intrinsic right to rule His creation. Those who labor or manage from such a posture are the real enemies of human dignity. They spoil the earth for the sake of money and reduce what once was a garden to a menacing jungle.

The image of the jungle is a metaphor used all too frequently to describe the business world. It harbors within it a distorted semblance to the original paradigm of the garden. Both are places of life and growth, but there the resemblance ends.

Where the garden exhibits symmetry and order, the jungle displays chaos. The jungle is a garden run wild, a place of violence and brutality. Where the garden is civilized and peaceful, the jungle is savage and barbarian. In the garden we carry the dignity of our humanity; in the jungle we become animals.

Wayne and Lefty had no illusions that a prayer breakfast would magically transform the corporate jungle into a garden. Their hope was that such an event would serve as a symbol to provoke awareness to the urgent need for men and women to see the practical relevance of God in the work world. Adopting the theme of "reconciliation," they set about the work of staging the event in Pittsburgh, a natural site for a peaceful meeting of labor and management.

Leadership for the breakfast was secured largely by the efforts of three men: John Guest, Reid Carpenter, and Robert Cleveland Holland. Guest, rector of St. Stephen's Episcopal Church in Sewickley, Pennsylvania, exposed his congregation to a special seminar on labor-management relations, thereby attracting several corporate executives to the event.

Reid Carpenter, a former Divisional Director of Young Life and active President of the Pittsburgh Leadership Foundation, was catalytic in involving the leadership of Pittsburgh in the breakfast. Carpenter, who had been "internally radicalized" by viewing Miracle of Pittron, said, "As I watched the story unfold on the screen, something happened to me inside. It dawned on me that if the work place is a jungle of conflict and hostility, the home life of the people involved could hardly be much different. The family was a secondary battleground."

Dr. Holland, whose commitment to the Value of the Person movement is deep, sponsored a second major seminar at the prestigious Shadyside Presbyterian Church. "To me, Wayne Alderson is a modern prophet, as important to the world of the working person as Martin Luther King was to the nation's blacks." Holland's support was so firm that he went through the rigorous process of nominating Wayne Alderson for a Templeton Foundation Award, presented annually by Prince Philip of

Cochairmen of the historic First Annual International Labor-Management Prayer Breakfast. George A. Stinson (left) and Lloyd McBride (right), with Wayne T. Alderson, Coordinator of the Breakfast. December 2, 1978.

England to the person the foundation judges to be the outstanding world figure in the field of religion.

With the help of Guest, Carpenter, and Holland, Alderson and Scumaci were able to enlist two internationally prominent leaders to be the cochairmen of the breakfast: George A. Stinson and Lloyd McBride.

George Stinson symbolizes the world of top-level management. As Chairman of the Board of National Steel Corporation, he functions as an elder statesman in the industrial world; his name is synonymous with success. Though burdened with involvement in numerous philanthropic projects, Stinson gave himself to the breakfast with earnest commitment. He personally contacted Lloyd McBride, International President of the United Steel Workers of America, and urged him to join him as cochairman of the event.

Lloyd McBride understands indignity, having suffered through the early years of ethnic discrimination in the job market. He has faced signs like "No Irish Need Apply"; he has been called "Shanty Irish," "Pig Shit Irish," and other terms that insult the people of St. Patrick. But he has transcended these, rejecting violent retaliation. He is at once tough and humorous, astute and sensitive. He responded to Stinson's request with warmth and enthusiasm.

The two met in an elegant office of the United Steel Workers Building, with its two walls of windows providing a panoramic view of the Golden Triangle; the men could view the mills and the barges as they joined hands in public affirmation of their mutual quest for labor peace.

An international prayer breakfast featuring men like McBride and Stinson captured the fancy of the press. Here were two giants of the industrial world—each representing forces that have historically been adversaries—coming together to publicly pray for peace. Both men are seasoned veterans of the wars between basic steel and the mammoth labor union of the United Steel Workers; both have a passion for the restoration of human dignity in the work world; both contradict the brutish image often painted of industrial tycoons and labor leaders; both exude a quiet dignity and sensitivity that might easily be mistaken for weakness. Yet both possess the enormous personal strength demanded of leaders of such powerful organizations. Their involvement was in no wise nominal. They were serious about this breakfast, risking their own reputations to cross an invisible line in behalf of recon-

Richard S. Caliguiri (left), Mayor of Pittsburgh, assisted by James W. Wilcock, Chairman and President of Joy Manufacturing Company, renames Liberty Avenue "Value of the Person" Street.

ciliation. Their example was duly noticed by their constituents.

The breakfast was greatly helped by a last-minute support effort led by Richard S. Caliguiri, Pittsburgh's dynamic, young mayor. Caliguiri, heir to the "Pittsburgh Renaissance" of urban renewal led by the David L. Lawrence "machine," had a heart for people. His dream was for "Renaissance II," a rebirth not so much of parks, streets, and buildings, but of the spirit of human dignity. The mayor issued a citywide proclamation declaring the week of November 25th, 1978, to be Value of the Person Week in Pittsburgh. The mayor followed the proclamation with a visible act of symbolism. He renamed Liberty Avenue, at the corner of Commonwealth, the Value of the Person Street.

The prayer breakfast actually began Friday night, December 1, 1978. The opening exercises found fifteen hundred people jamming the Ballroom of the Pittsburgh Hilton. The speakers platform included McBride, Stinson, Piccolo, and a host of dignitaries. The following morning saw the main event, with remarks offered by Senator John Heinz, Governor Richard Thornburgh, Mayor Caliguiri, Shirley Carr of Canada, and others. United States Secretary of Labor Ray Marshal delivered greetings to the participants from President Carter, in which the President expressed his delight with the breakfast by a formal communiqué. These were the preliminaries—the main address was to be given by Wayne Alderson.

Wayne's stomach was churning as he waited his turn. His eyes swept across the audience, taking note of the strange admixture of blue collar workers seated at the same tables as corporate executives. He took comfort from seeing his two sisters, Jeanne and Lil, seated next to his nephew and namesake. Young Wayne had already recapitulated Alderson's own life in one important respect—he was seriously wounded in Vietnam at the age of eighteen.

Alderson was introduced by the aged black chipper from Pittron, Deacon Lunsford. As he stepped to the podium, the steel worker embraced Wayne in an affectionate bear hug, hanging on tightly with fierce emotion. When Deacon hugged him like that, his mind snapped back to the trench. The only other man who ever hugged him that way was Red Preston. It was a death grip, and he felt the same thing from Deacon. "I just had to talk about Red," Wayne recalled, "because that's where the Value of the Person was born for me. My hatred for war welled up in me and I had to talk about peace."

Among the speakers at the prayer breakfast were: Vince Slavik, Laborer, United Steelworkers of America at Pittron (top left). Sam Piccolo, former President of United Steelworkers of America Local 1306 and presently USWA District 15 Staff Representative (top right). Francis "Lefty" Scumaci, Director, Office, Technical and Professional Workers of the United Steelworkers of America (bottom left). Reid Carpenter, former Young Life Director and presently President of the Pittsburgh Leadership Foundation (bottom right).

Wayne began his speech in tones one writer described as "a vanilla pudding voice." For the first time in public, he recounted his experiences with Red Preston at the Siegfried Line. Alderson spoke of economic warfare in the work world, and ended his address with a challenge issued to each group represented there:

"I say to the churches, quit hiding underneath your steeples. Come off your reservation and send God's people into the work world to live for God.

"I say to government and people in the political arena, stop being politicians looking to the next election. It's time to start being statesmen, looking to the next generation.

"I say to labor and management leaders, give us what we want . . . a leadership style of reconciliation."

After the breakfast, the participants broke into seminar groups to focus attention on special problems confronting the work world. One examined the growing militance of Marxist attempts to infiltrate the American work force.

A primary strategy of the Marxists is to reach the masses of working people, the "exploited proletariat" with a vision and promise of a better life. This strategy has been successful as a catalyst for revolution in many countries. The United States is not exempt from or immune to that strategy.

Marx viewed private property and wages as the twin causes of all human social estrangement. The abolishment of private property is still the kernel of the Marxist dream that promises the utopia of a classless society with an equal distribution of wealth.

But the Marxist dream is a nightmare. The track record of proletariat revolutions is one of agonizing tyranny. Yet people still try it, and converts are won every day. When workers lose their sense of dignity, when they are not valued, they become vulnerable to the empty promises of Marxism. Alderson's vision of reformation is a conscious alternative to violent revolution. He takes the Marxist threat seriously, working to correct the problems that create an atmosphere of frustration for the worker and leave him susceptible to the Marxist myth. Alderson knows that someone will inevitably fill the void that is not being addressed by labor and management.

Another seminar featured Alderson speaking of the crisis of productivity in industry. The gloomy statistics of the spiraling decline in America's productivity improvement rate to a zero growth rate are numbers that management men understand. Pittron's amazing 64 percent productivity improvement rate sparked the repeated question to Alderson, "How did you do it?"

Wayne argued that productivity must be seen as a byproduct of valuing people. Succinctly, he cut the gordian knot of discussion with these words: "Government cannot *legislate* productivity; labor cannot *negotiate* productivity; arbitrators cannot *mediate* productivity; management cannot *intimidate* productivity; scholars cannot *educate* productivity; and churches cannot *proclamate* productivity." Productivity cannot be bought. Incentive plans, government programs, and special study groups have evidently failed to deal with the problem. For Alderson, it is a "people problem. The great ecological issue," he says, "is not the problem of the natural resources of water, land, coal or oil. It is a problem of our most precious natural resource, our people. The solution to the productivity problem must be found in how we treat people."

The prayer breakfast piqued the interest of the press. That men like Stinson and McBride would join forces publicly in prayer for the work world was news. NBC's Pittsburgh affiliate, WIIC, filmed the entire event and later produced a thirty-minute special documentary on it. CBS featured four minutes of coverage on its national Evening News with Walter Cronkite. Positive reports were printed in *Industry Week* and the *Wall Street Journal.* AP and UPI covered the story on their wires.

One publication, however, responded with open hostility. On Thursday, December 7, 1978, the *Daily World* (which replaced the *Daily Worker* as the chief organ of the American Communist Party) used two-inch high headlines to herald its feature article: *BOSSES LAUNCH ANTI-LABOR CULT.*

Denouncing Alderson and the prayer breakfast, the *Daily World* referred to it as a "pseudo-religious productivity cult," likening Alderson to the founder of Jonestown. The article described the event as a management-inspired gimmick designed to lull the workers into being fooled and exploited.

The Communist Party was not the only group antagonistic to Alderson. Though the breakfast solidified new support for the Value of the Person movement, it also brought new opposition. Threats against Alderson increased and some radical groups stepped up their attacks. The far left within the unions accused him of being pro management, while the far right within management accused him of being pro-union.

A growing number of corporations have been hiring professional consultants whose principle talents are devoted to union-busting, a goal of those who are committed to a "union-free environment." Because Alderson practices as a management consultant, he is vulnerable to attempts to be used or prostituted. One large industrial complex had resisted requests by some of their leaders to employ Alderson for training sessions at one of their strategic non-union plants. When, for the first time in the plant's long history, the rank and file got enough signatures for a vote for organization, the plant officials suddenly called Wayne and requested that he give a training seminar on the Value of the Person. Wayne asked the obvious question: "Why do you want me now?"

The official responded matter of factly, "We want to defeat the vote to organize the unions." Wayne was furious that such an overt attempt to prostitute him was being made.

His refusal made him open to the charge of being anti-management. The fine line he tries to walk is thus often obliterated by those committed to the adversary relationship between labor and management. Alderson insists that he is neither pro-labor nor pro-management, but pro-people. He is critical of management when it fails to treat labor with dignity and re-

spect; he is equally critical when union members have no respect for management. The adversary syndrome goes well beyond the labor-management struggle. Alderson is aware of the
adversary relationship that exists between the unionized
worker and the non-union worker. Frequently, the most hated
enemy of organized labor is not management, but the non-
union worker who is treated with contempt and known by the
demeaning nickname of "scab." Alderson seeks for reconciliation in this battleground as well.

Reid Carpenter interviewed one corporate executive who
attended the breakfast at the request of his partner. Reid asked
him, "Would you come if Alderson had invited you?"

"No," was the sharp reply. "I don't trust him . . . he can't be
controlled."

Here the words were spoken openly. "He can't be controlled"—the very reason some management men won't trust
him is the reason so many of the rank and file do trust him. This
obstinate refusal to be controlled by either side is what evokes
ire from some and admiration from others.

Wayne Alderson is not a professional philosopher, chained to
a desk in a musty library. He is a visionary of the grass roots, a
prophet in the marketplace. Not content with the way things
are, he dreams of a better world.

Sometimes dreamers use their reverie as an escape tunnel
from responsibility, content to offer a blurred vision fortified by
dry martinis while the world is in flames. Such dreamers are
relatively harmless, disturbing no one with their utopian fantasies. Their lives are lived within the boundaries of their own
heads; their dreams are the secrets of Walter Mitty.

Other dreamers become dangerous. When their dream life is
frustrated by brutal reality they become enraged. Unable to
tolerate the loss of paradise, they turn their dreams into ugly
acts of violence. Some even entice others into a ring of hatred,
committing themselves to a policy of wanton destruction. They
become radicals, violent revolutionaries, promising dreams but
producing nightmares. Men like the Bavarian corporal who

spent too much time in jail writing *Mein Kampf* go berserk seeking to impose their dreams on the masses. The record of history is full of the evil unleashed on the world by such "dreamers," who charge against a flaming world armed with gasoline. Theirs is a policy of confrontation.

But there is another kind of dreamer, the kind who tempers his dream with a quiet understanding that, for the dream to become reality, it requires disciplined work. Such a dreamer recognizes that though all is not right with the world, all is not wrong with it either. This kind of dreamer is not so foolish as to think he is a God who can create a new order by his own divine imperative. He knows that he, himself, is an integral part of the imperfection of the world, and that even his own dream may add to that imperfection. This kind of dreamer works for daily improvement, knowing that it is impossible for anyone ever to create the world afresh.

Alderson is such a man, a radical not in the wild pejorative sense, but in the classic sense of the word—one who seeks to go to the *radix*, the root, of the problem. His dream is not of revolution, but of reformation. He sees the wide chasm that exists between reform and revolt. He rejects the revolt motif that attacks all present structures.

Alderson is a "qualified capitalist." He is of that generation (perhaps merely a vestigial appendage) which believes that the United States, with all of its present weaknesses and struggles is still a "noble experiment." Alderson never equates America with the Kingdom of God, nor does he embrace a kind of civil religion where the flag is adored in an apotheosis of the state. But he cherishes the virtues of economic and political freedom.

Alderson's "qualified" capitalism rejects both the virulent form of unrestrained *lassez faire capitalism,* which lives on a survival of the fittest mentality, and *socialistic capitalism,* in which the term "private enterprise" becomes a euphemism for virtual government ownership achieved by high levels of taxation and regulation. Alderson puts a pox on both these economic houses. He rejects the former because it justifies economic oppression by the rich and powerful under the deceptive cloak of free enterprise. It guarantees economic freedom for the "haves" and economic and political oppression for the "have nots,"—slaves don't ever vote. He rejects the latter because government interference strangles the businessman as the corporation can barely breathe as it is surrounded, thwarted, and frustrated by regulations. In this system government, not labor, becomes industry's highest form of overhead. Socialistic capitalism moves inexorably in the direction of government ownership. Government ownership operates on the principle that everybody owns everything, which means that nobody owns anything. Private ownership then becomes a myth of the state.

Alderson's brand of capitalism is drawn from the biblical concept of *stewardship.* The stewardship principle assumes the *right to private ownership* (protected by the Ten Commandments, which include prohibitions against stealing and coveting); the right of *capital investment,* and most importantly, the principle of *ownership with responsibility.*

The New Testament word for stewardship is *oikonomos* (from which the word "economy" is derived). The word combines two Greek roots, *oikos* (house) and *nomos* (law). The biblical "steward" is the "house ruler," the person who possesses the house, rules the house, and is responsible for the well-being of the house. In creation, man is made the steward of the created order. He is given "dominion" over the earth, with the divinely ordained mandate to "dress, till, and keep" the earth and to "replenish it." It means that greed must never be a license for exploitive practices "justified" by profits. In other words, private property and commerce are to be governed by laws—laws which are according to righteousness. God Himself gives content to that righteousness. The "justice" of divine *oikonomia* is not defined by lobby groups, vested interest legislation, or "law of the jungle" theories. The justice of Christian economics is determined by the standard of righteousness revealed in God's word. God grants the gifts of material goods and regulates that material order by His law. This is not "free" enterprise in the sense of human autonomy. All people are accountable to God for the way in which they acquire, market, and use their goods.

As an advocate of stewardship capitalism, Alderson is convinced that the ideals of love, dignity, and respect have a vital place in corporate life. What happened at Pittron proved that such virtues are eminently practical. The problem focuses on overcoming the prejudices, the blind spots of both labor and management traditions, produced by years of perpetuating uncritically accepted assumptions. Alderson searches for ways to give the human factor in the work place more visibility, for ways of awakening industry to the urgent issues of human dignity.

From the first international prayer breakfast in 1978, through the second in 1979, Wayne Alderson has continued to crisscross the nation, speaking, leading seminars, showing the film, and dialoging with students, church groups, and leaders of labor and management. A growing body of people have been awakened to new hope for labor peace and stability.

In March of 1980, President Jimmy Carter made a dramatic announcement of a new program to combat the crisis of an inflation rate racing toward twenty percent annually. He called for a balanced budget, reduction in foreign oil imports, and a reversal in our declining rate of productivity.

A few days after his national announcement, President Carter dispatched a special envoy to the Steel Valley of western Pennsylvania to meet with Wayne Alderson. Presidential advisor Dr. Robert Maddox met with Wayne and a group of Value of the Person advocates in the union hall of USWA Local 1306, the home local of Sam Piccolo and the men of Pittron. The conference took place only steps from the entrance to the giant steel foundry now owned by Bucyrus-Erie.

After a brief address in which Dr. Maddox expressed his feelings about being in a union hall for the first time in his life, he opened the floor to the audience, saying, "Please tell me what you would like the President to know. How can we help?"

Maddox displayed a spirit of compassion as he touched and was touched in the heart by those present. The men of Pittron spoke up. One said, "You're worried about productivity. We are all producers. Give us dignity and you'll get all the production you need."

A twenty-one-year-old chipper, Tim Dick, responded, "I wear a Value of the Person pin in the mill. It reminds me not to get angry or cynical. Everybody asks about it, but not enough people know about it. Help us get the message out."

Mike Bonn, President of Local 2227, said, "Get the film on national tv. Let the people see what can happen everywhere because of what happened here."

Perhaps the most passionate words were spoken by Paul Lewis, District 15 Director, USWA: "Dr. Maddox, you talk with our leaders in Washington; maybe you can even influence new legislation. But what we're talking about doesn't need new legislation, it's already there. About 205 years ago our fathers wrote some guidelines down on paper. When the world heard of them, people flocked here for freedom, for economic opportunity, and for dignity. Words penned in 1776 were like a splash on a crystal clear pond, sending waves across the water. But the further away they moved, the ripples became weaker and weaker and weaker. Now we can't even see them.

"At Gettysburg our President stood up and reminded the nation of those words—'For the people.' He had to speak because the value of people had been forgotten. Had we done what we said we were going to do, there would have been no Gettysburg Address, because there would not have been a battlefield there to provide such a speech. Why do we need a Martin Luther King Day? Why do we have an issue about bussing? Because we didn't do our job in the first place.

"The Value of the Person is not new. We need to dust off the history books and read the story again. Our fathers made far greater sacrifices than we are making—not for profit, but for an ideal, the value of people. It wasn't even new then, they didn't invent it, it was already in the Bible. But those men chose to write it in our Constitution. It's all in our archives, but it's not in our land.

"It has taken 205 years for another person to come forward and say it again. I never met Thomas Jefferson, but I do know Wayne Alderson. He is simply saying the same thing."

Alderson added: "We're talking about changing attitudes, the hardest thing in the world to change. We need something stronger than legislation, stronger than government programs. Today words like love, dignity, and respect are considered weak words. They're not. Those words have strength, they're stronger than steel."

Three days later President and Rosalyn Carter met with Robert Maddox at Camp David to view the film and consider ways to bring the Value of the Person to the nation.

Though the printed page may make a man seem bigger than life, the fact remains that Wayne Alderson is a common man, living out the legacy of the coal fields. He is not a child of privilege or wealth, a "wunderkind" with prodigious natural talent. In most respects he is a simple man. Yet all simple men are at the same time complex, as all complex personalities are at the same time simple. Alderson's dream of dignity for working people is not uncommon. His frustration with destructive business practices is not uncommon. His love of peace is not uncommon. His courage to venture out to the point, to call for reformation *is* uncommon. The sacrificial heroism of Red Preston left an indelible mark on Wayne Alderson. Red Preston was a common man who performed an uncommon act. That's what drives Wayne—a consummate desire to encourage men and women to make the uncommon, commonplace.

# Epilogue

The decade of the sixties marked one of the most turbulent periods of unrest in American history, almost surpassing the great schism of the Civil War and the bleak mood of the Depression. The sixties were the "angry years," punctuated by epidemic protests.

In the seventies the protest movements of the previous decade ran out of gas. So did the nation. The energy crisis, coupled with inflation and the international devaluation of the dollar, awakened a new popular interest in basic economics. The news reports now featured commentaries on the price of gold rather than the latest body count in Vietnam.

The eighties were ushered in by international turmoil erupting in trouble spots with strong ties to nations crucial to international energy sources. Terrorism in Iran and the Soviet invasion of Afghanistan brought new perils to international economics. The rest of the eighties is before us, issuing a challenge to our national future. The outcome is shrouded in doubt. Whether America will be a survivor of the eighties is uncertain. What is certain is that the present unrest in the work world must be resolved. American industry is faced with the prospect of an ugly worker uprising, foreshadowed by the storming of U. S. Steel Headquarters by protesting workers in December of 1979. Reformation is no longer an optional luxury, it is a necessity.

A work-world reformation will require uncommon courage. The Church must be willing to come off the reservation, taking its values into the marketplace. The people of God must plug their ears to the voices of the cynics and skeptics. Reformations of society are never accomplished by the intimidated.

In themselves, men like Wayne Alderson belong to the ranks of the powerless. Yet they are called to take on the powerful. They are handicapped by limiting their weapons to those of peace. Rejecting violence, terrorism, and other tactics of intimidation, they are left only with spiritual means of combat sanctioned by God Himself.

For those like Alderson, a trip to the point may be suicidal. Jobs may indeed be lost and casualties real. But it is not necessarily so. Men like Sam Piccolo and Lefty Scumaci have taken large risks. They have not been fired. In fact, they have been rewarded. Both have been given significant promotions by the USWA—Lefty to the position of director of the Office, Technical, and Professional Workers, and Sam to the position of staff representative. Both now move in the upper échelons of the USWA, vindicated for their efforts in behalf of worker dignity.

In its April 28, 1980, issue, *Business Week* magazine highlighted the new provisions of a historic basic steel-labor settlement. The article, garnished with action photos of Lefty Scumaci and Joe Odercich (who replaced the hospitalized Lloyd McBride as chief negotiator), stated:

Perhaps more important, the settlement may signal a fundamental shift in steel's labor relations—away from traditional adversary confrontation between workers and bosses and toward a more cooperative approach to common problems in the workplace.

Alderson is still out on the point, encouraging others to join him, calling upon them to make the uncommon commonplace. His challenge is one we dare not ignore.

"We have tried man's way. It has failed. Now it is time to try God's way."

# Index